I0446502

THIS BOOK BELONGS TO

For permissions requests, contact the publisher at ooffoopub@gmail.com.

Published by OOFFOO Publications.

Test Your Color Here

Test Your Color Here

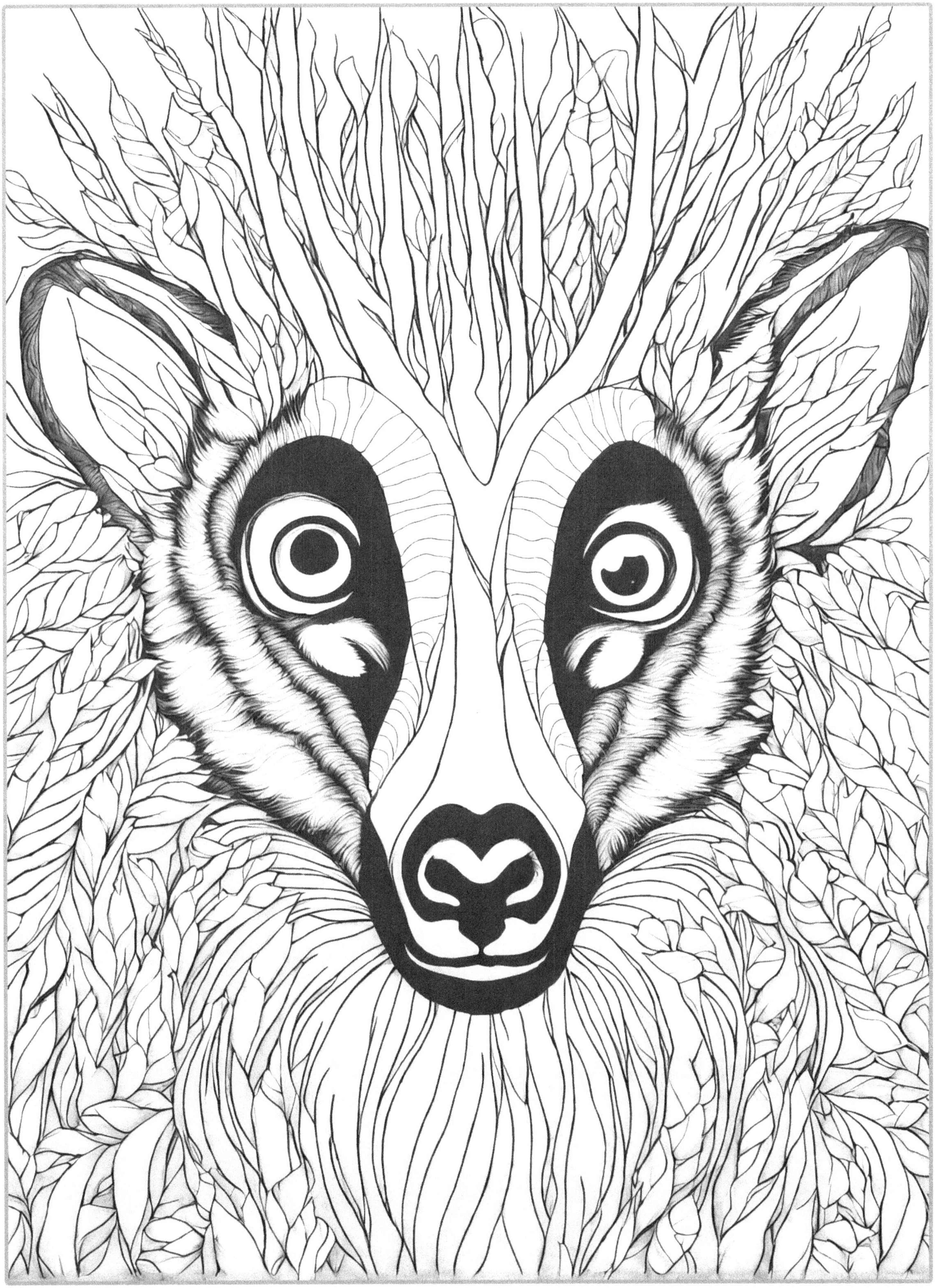

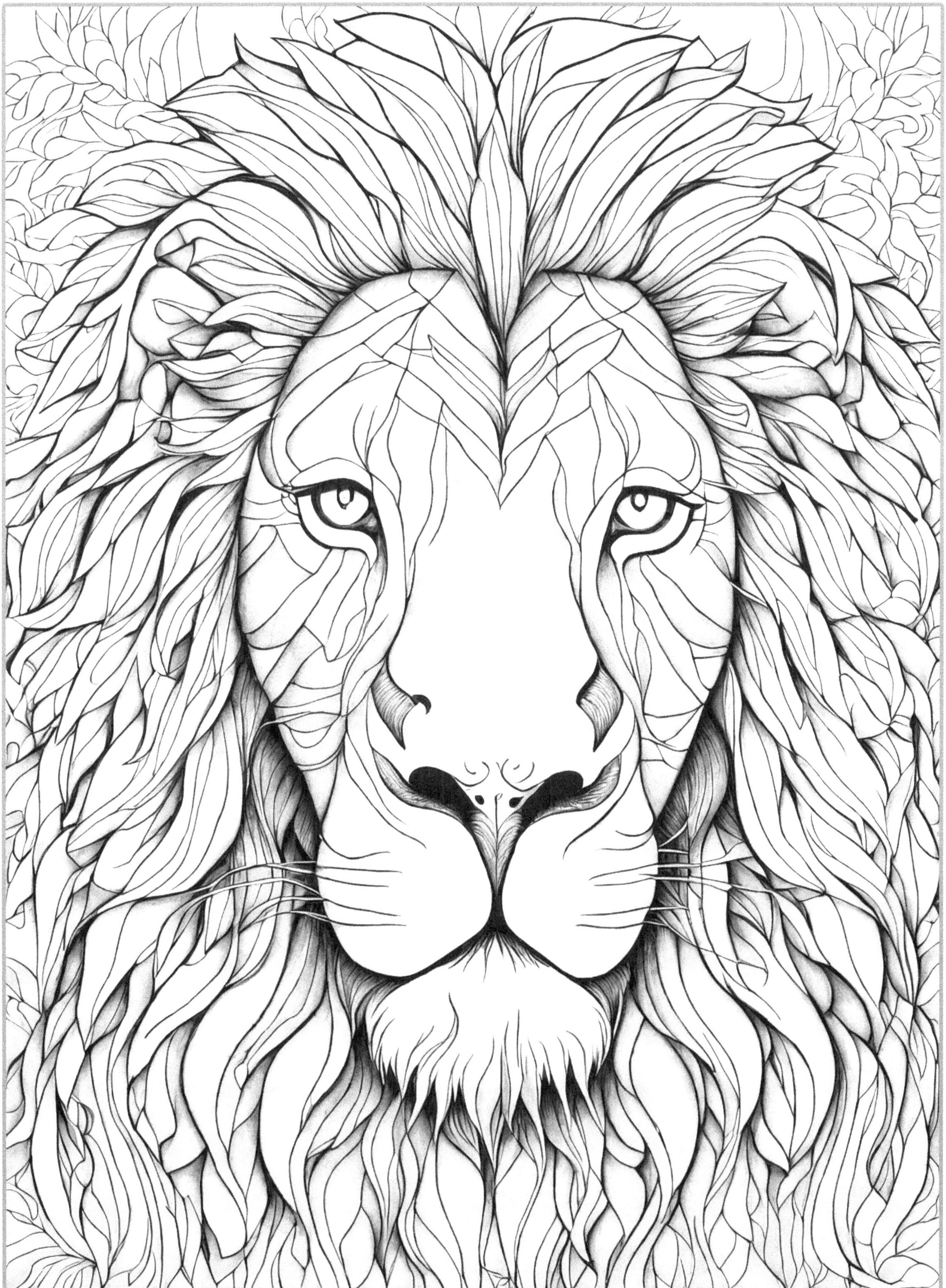

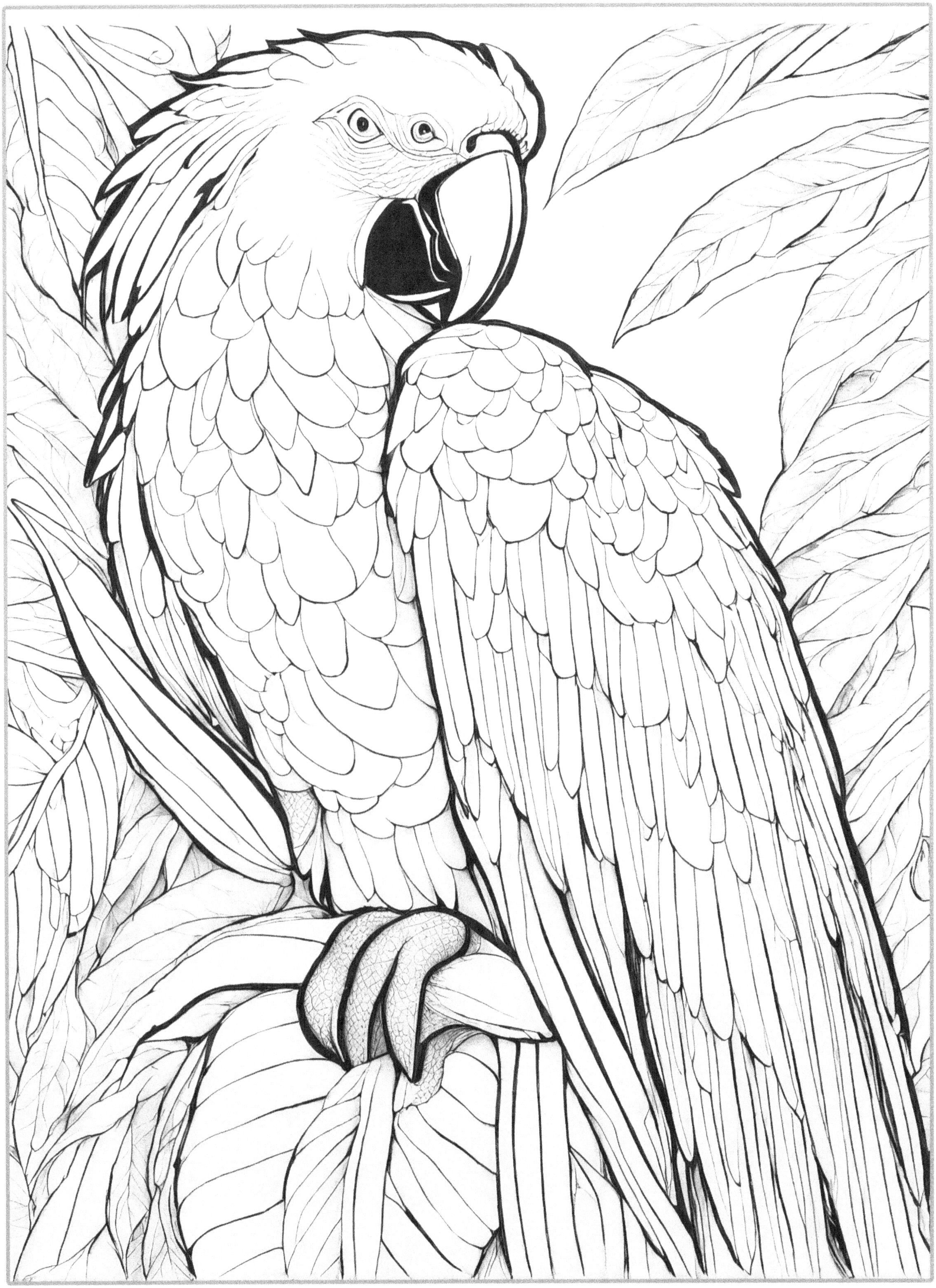

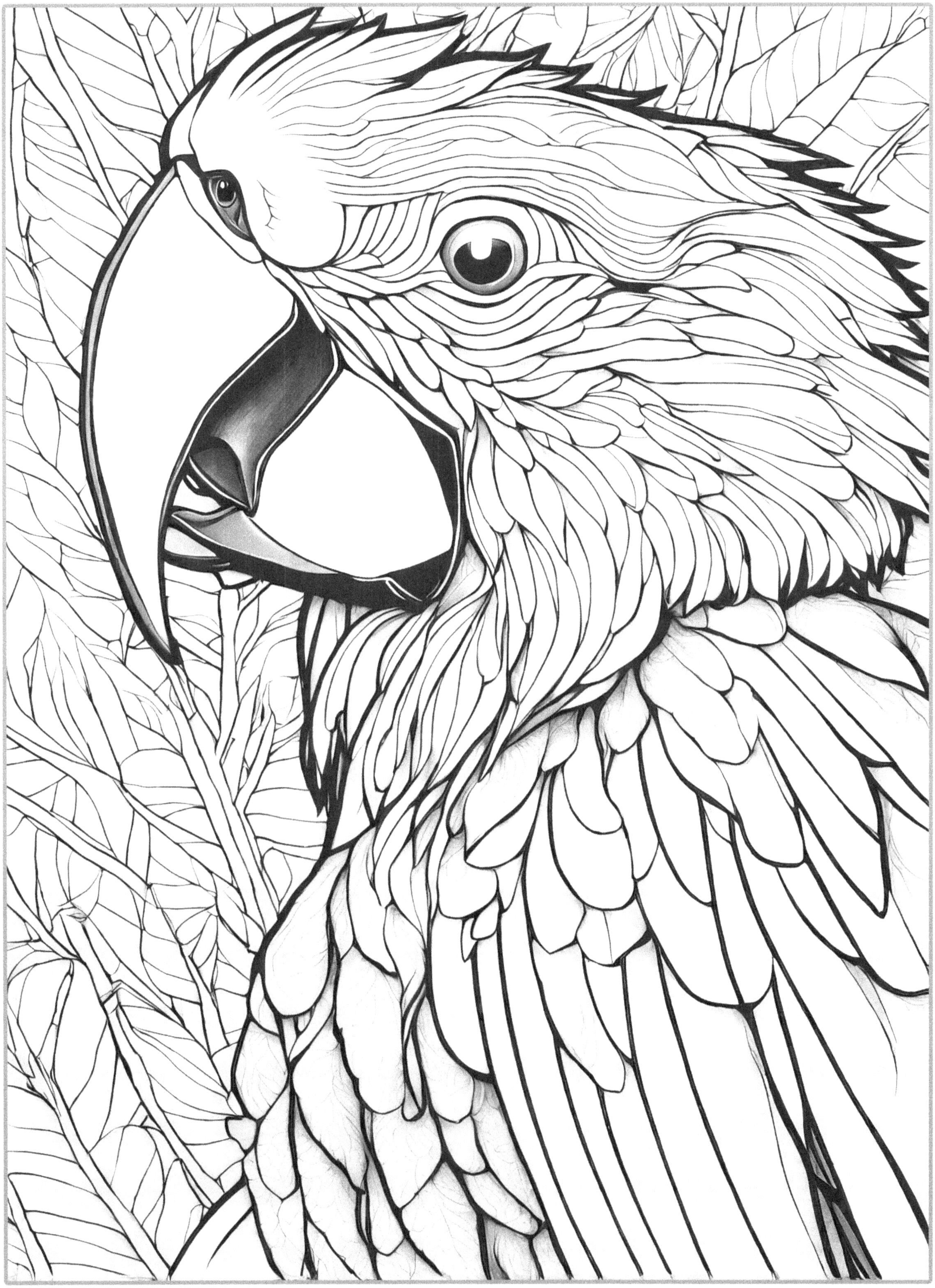

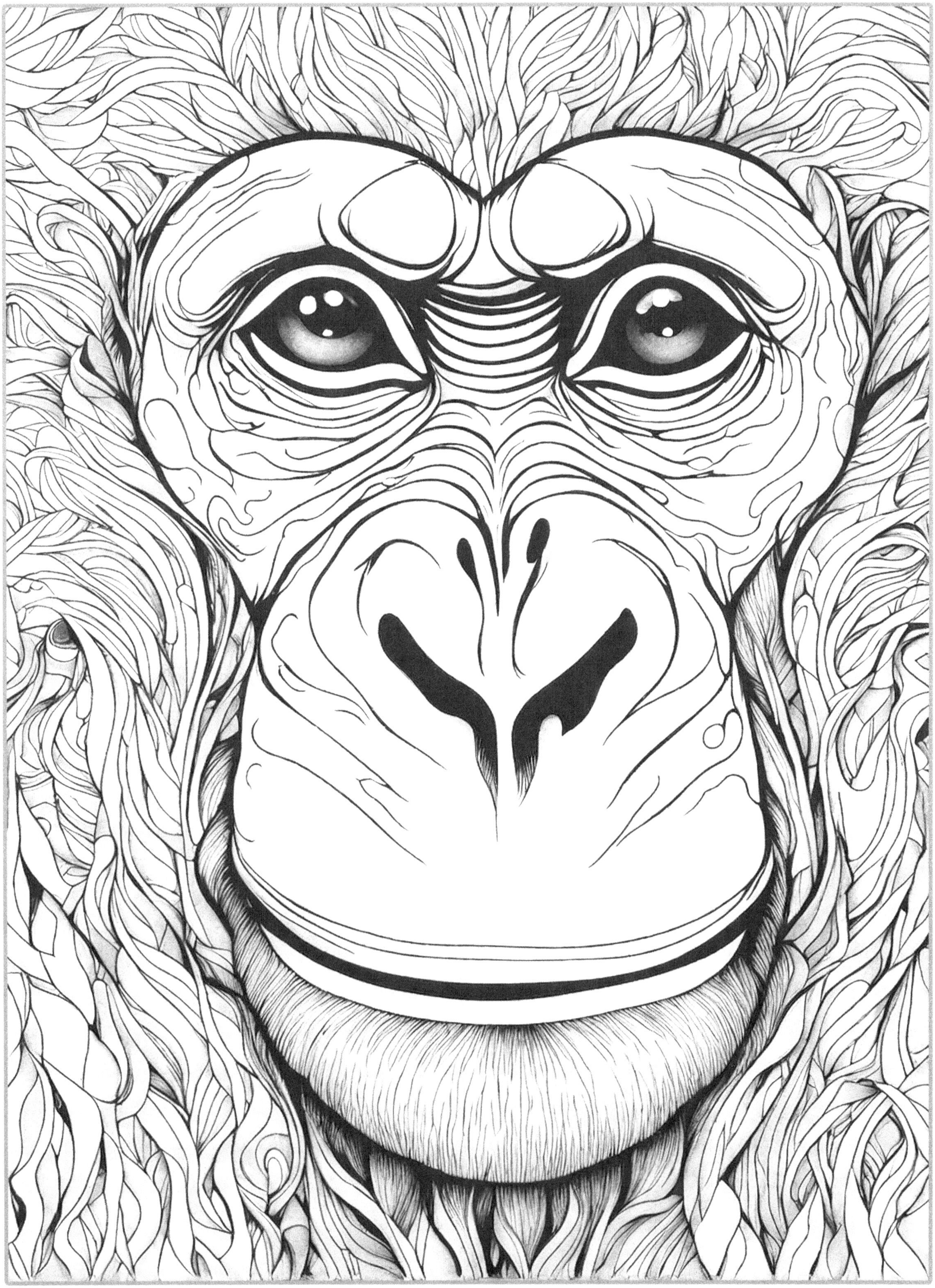

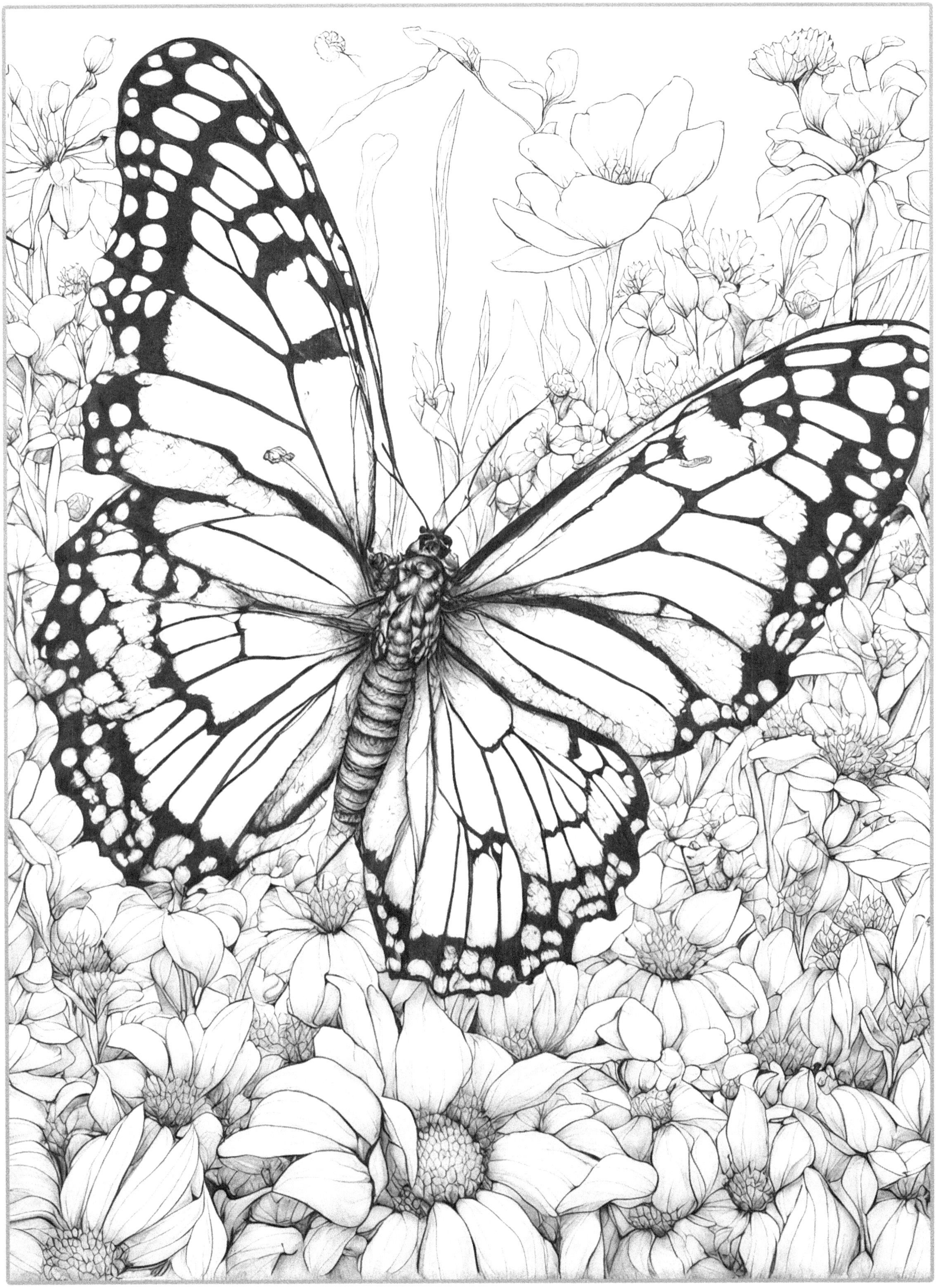

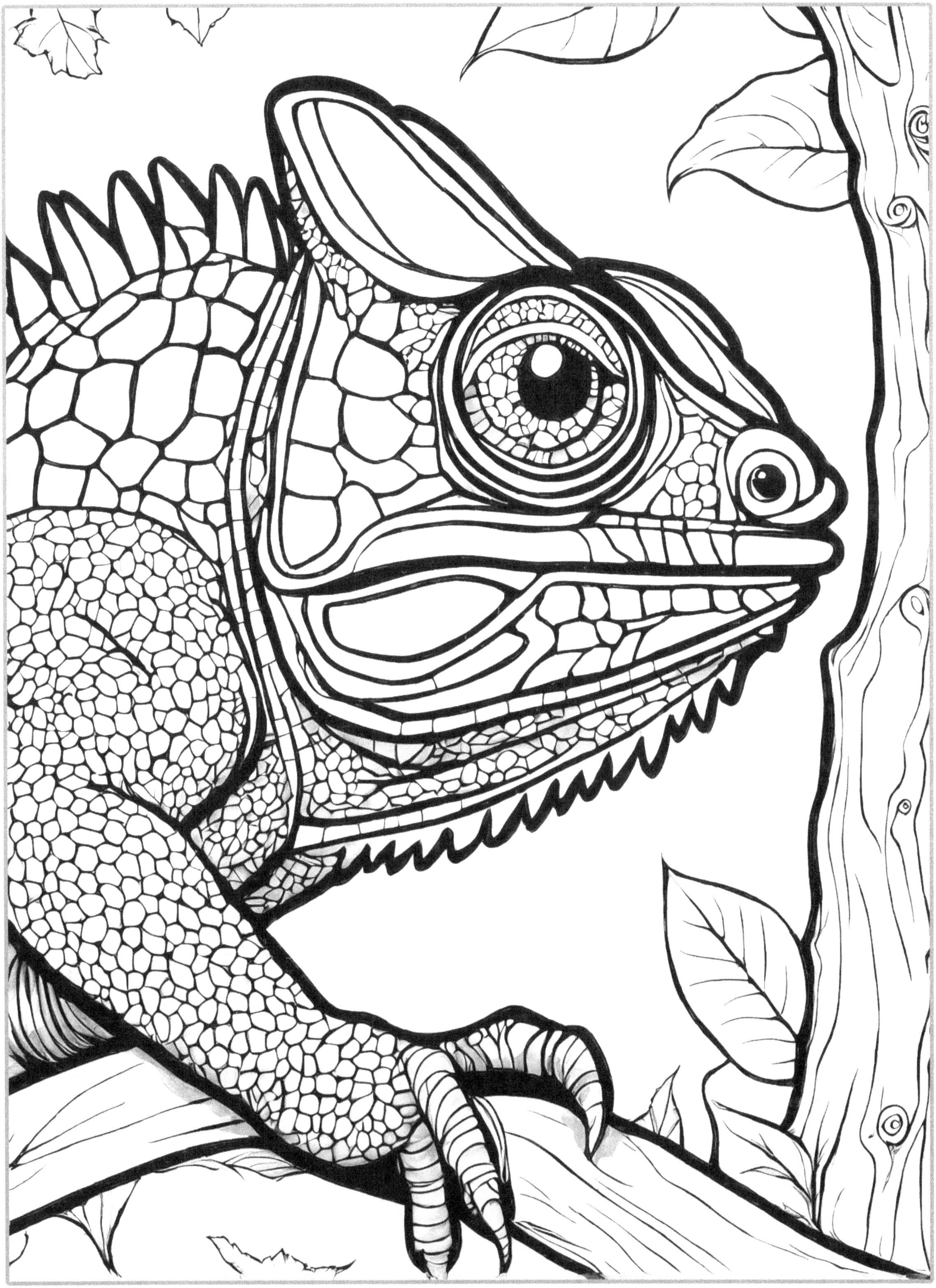

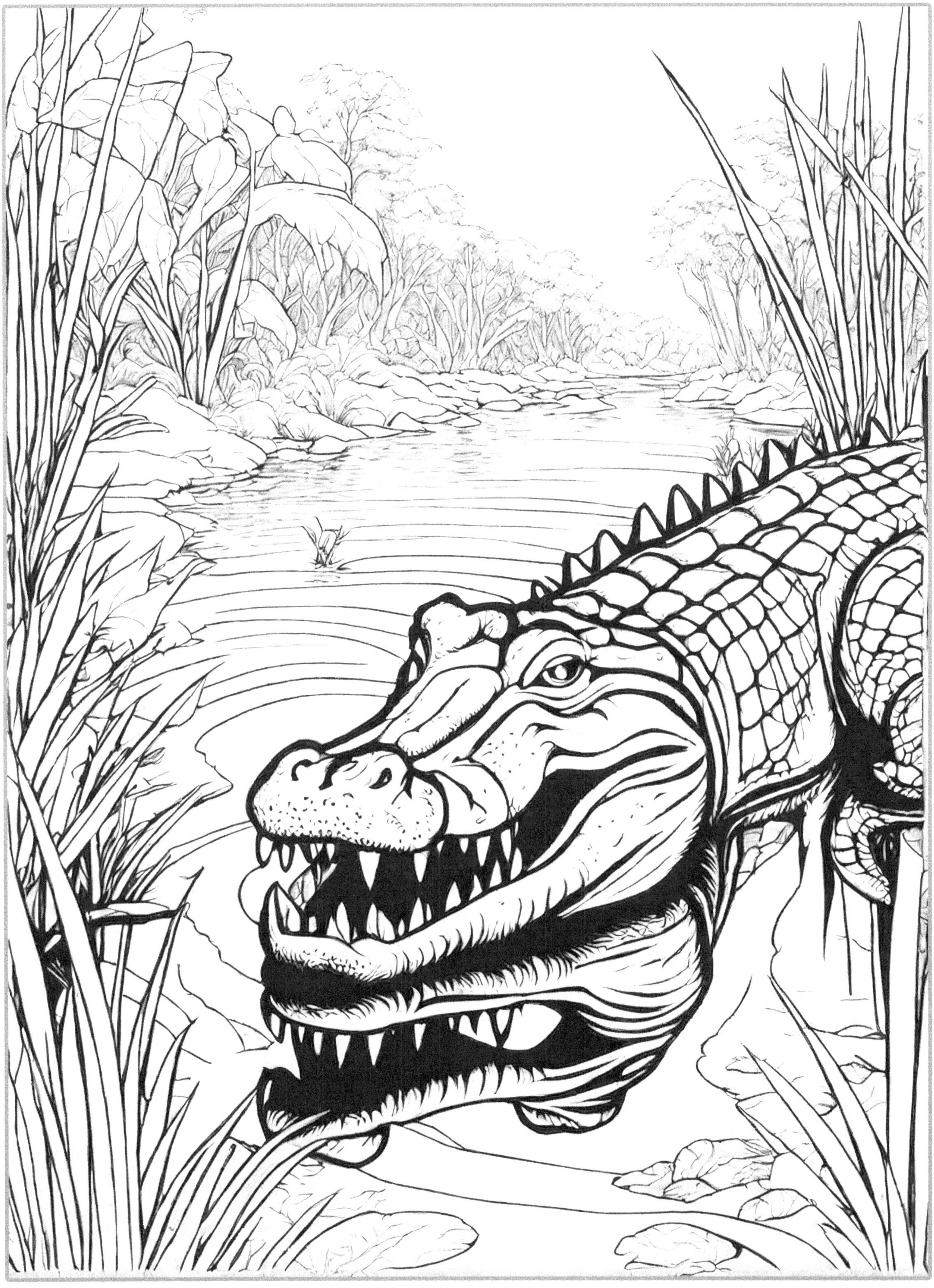

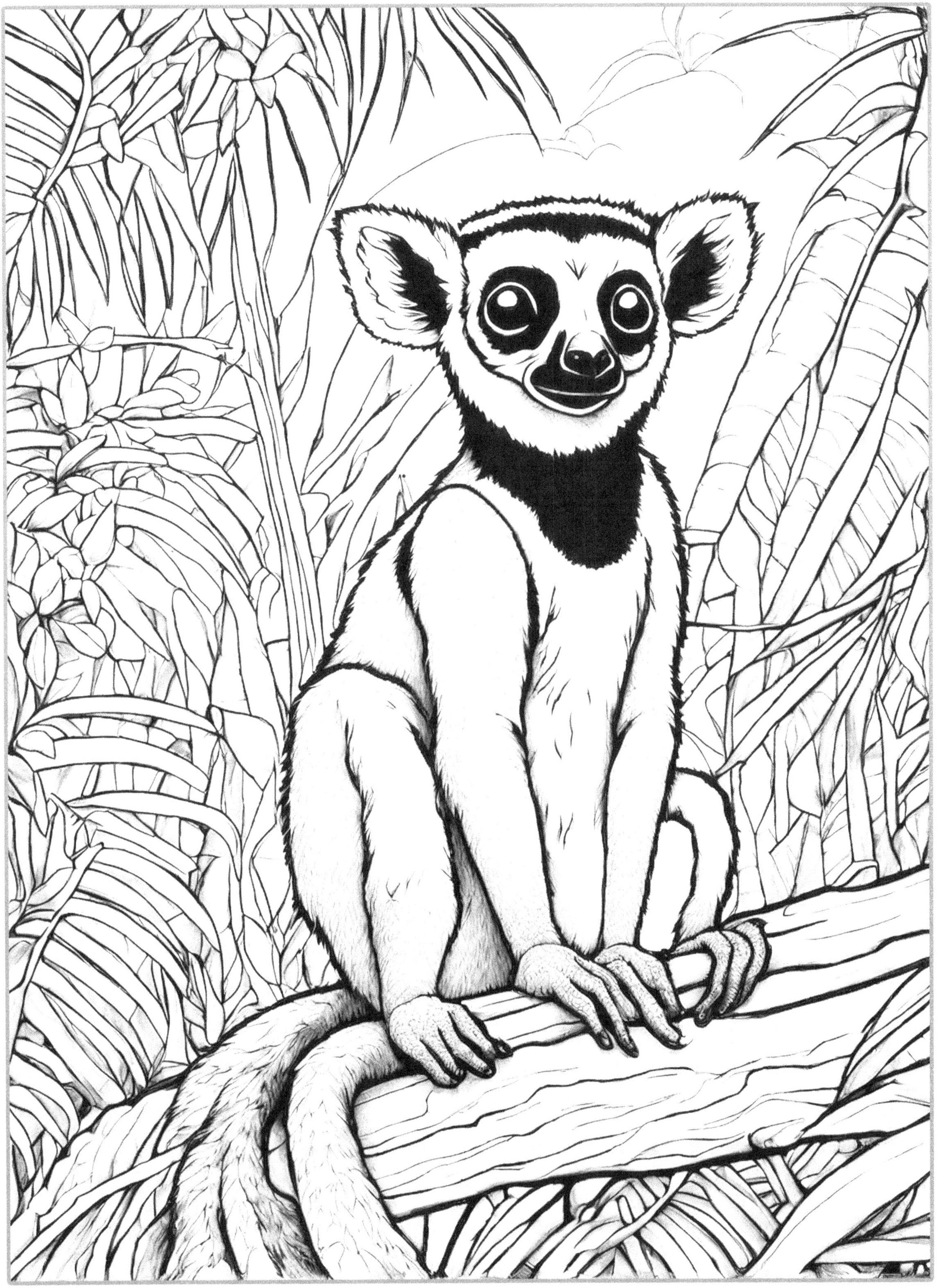

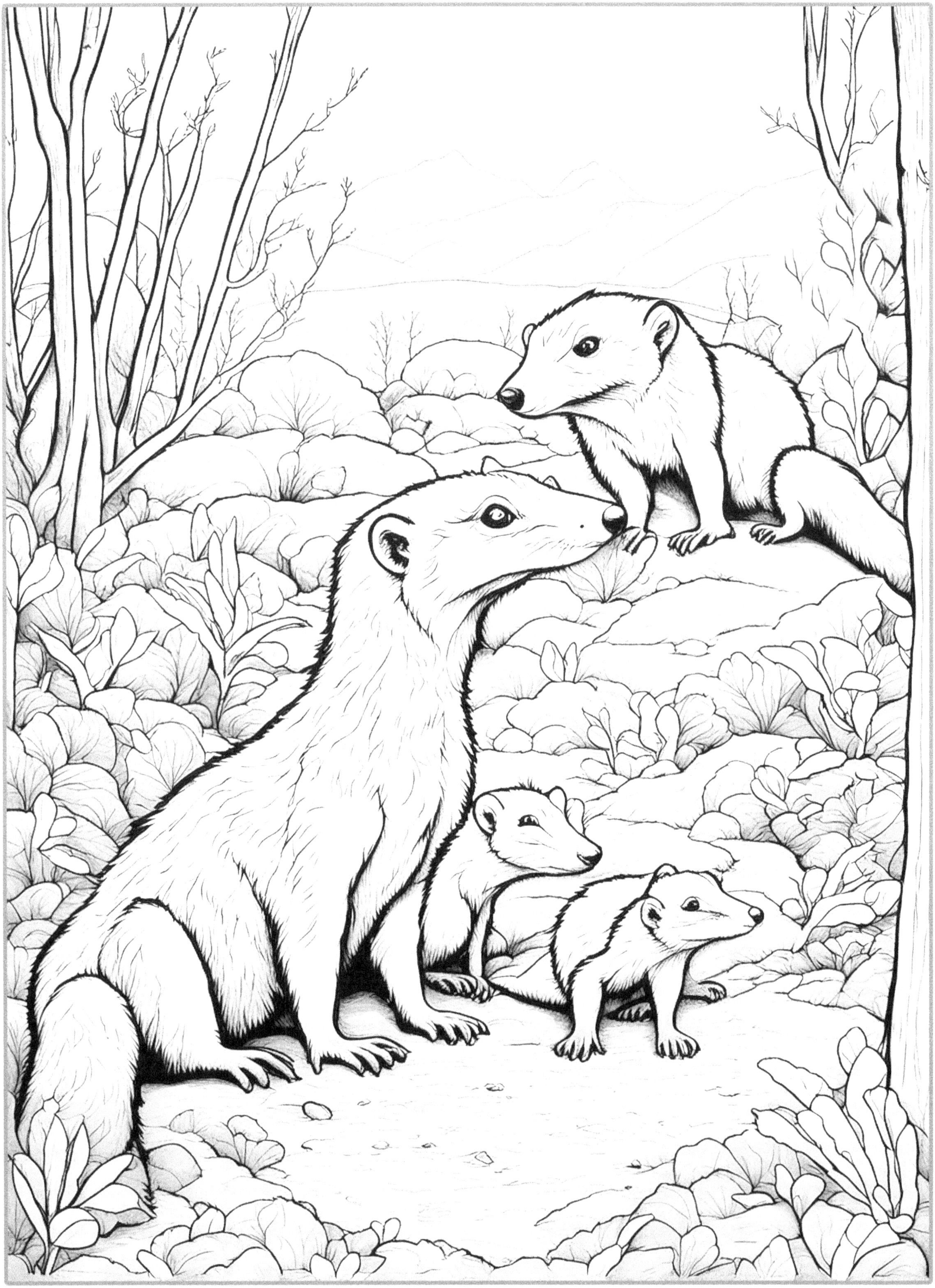

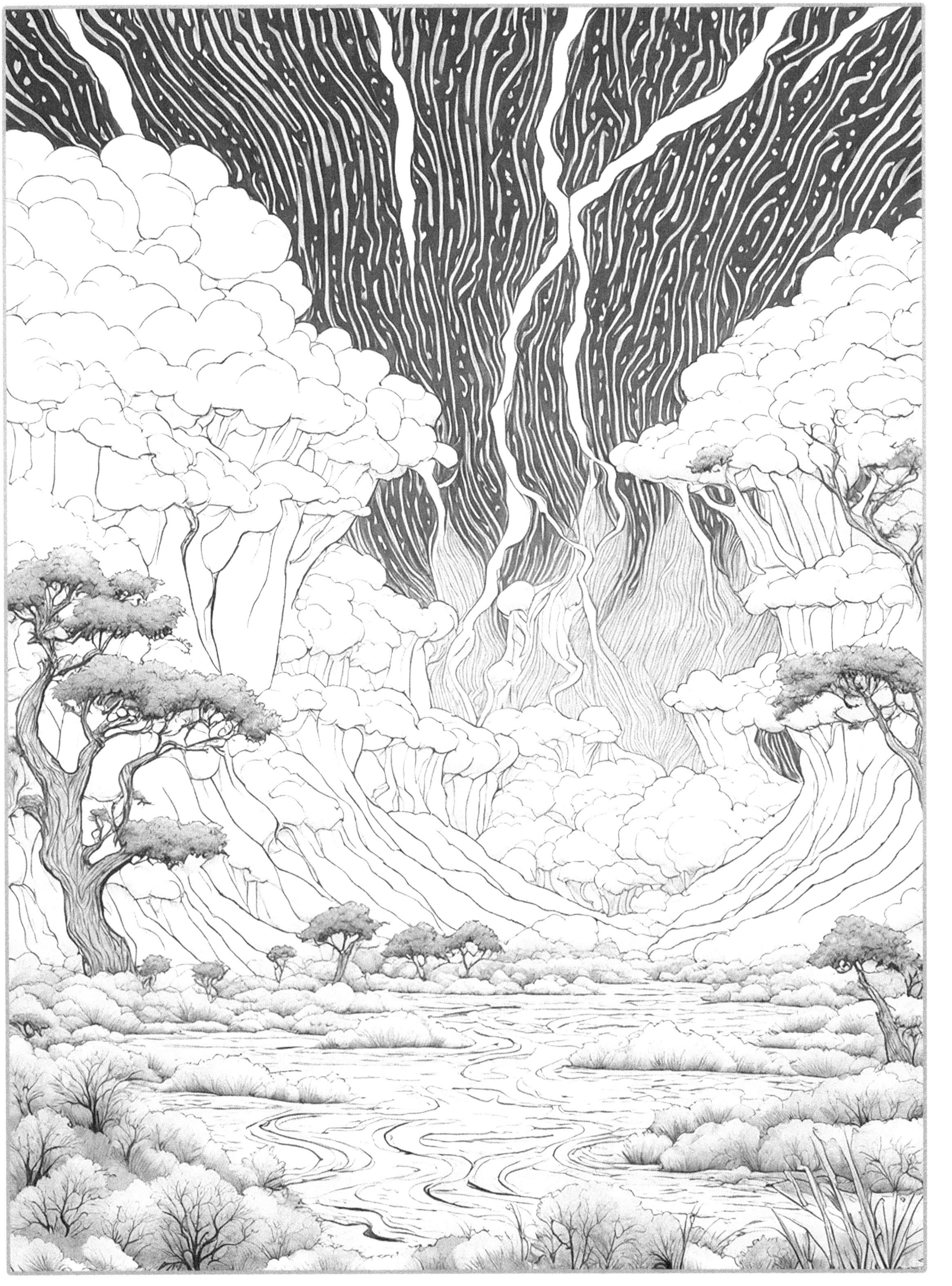

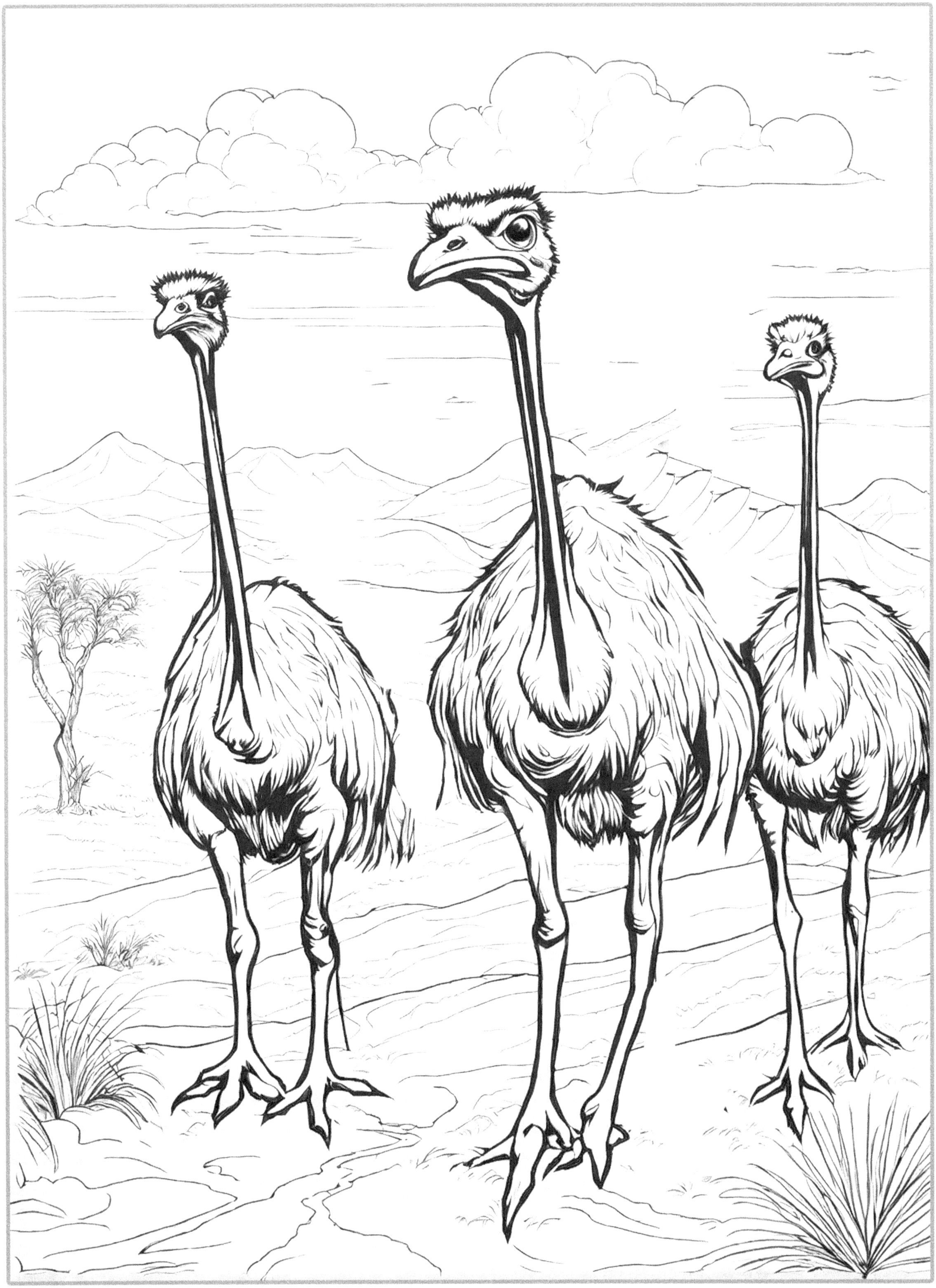

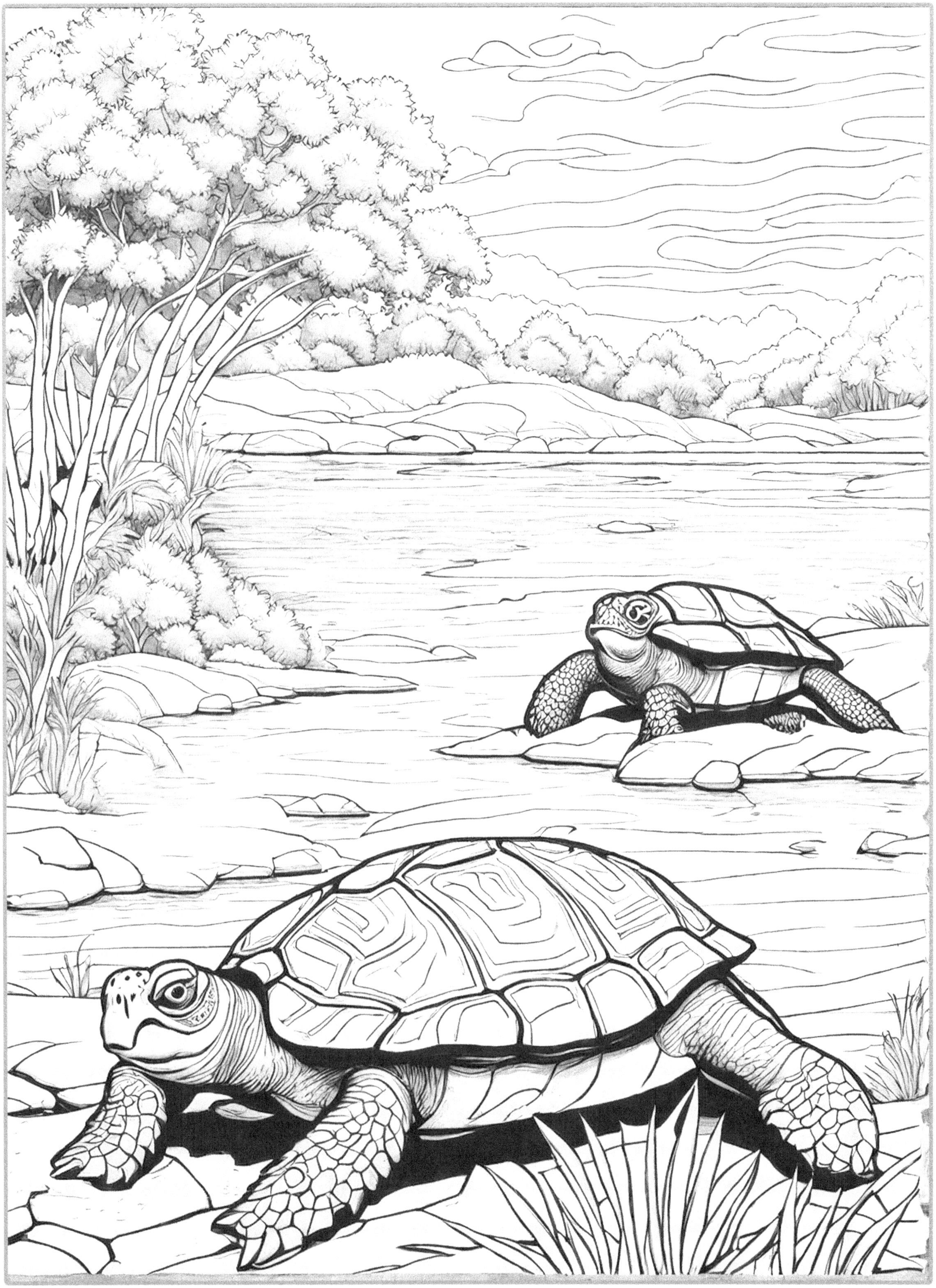

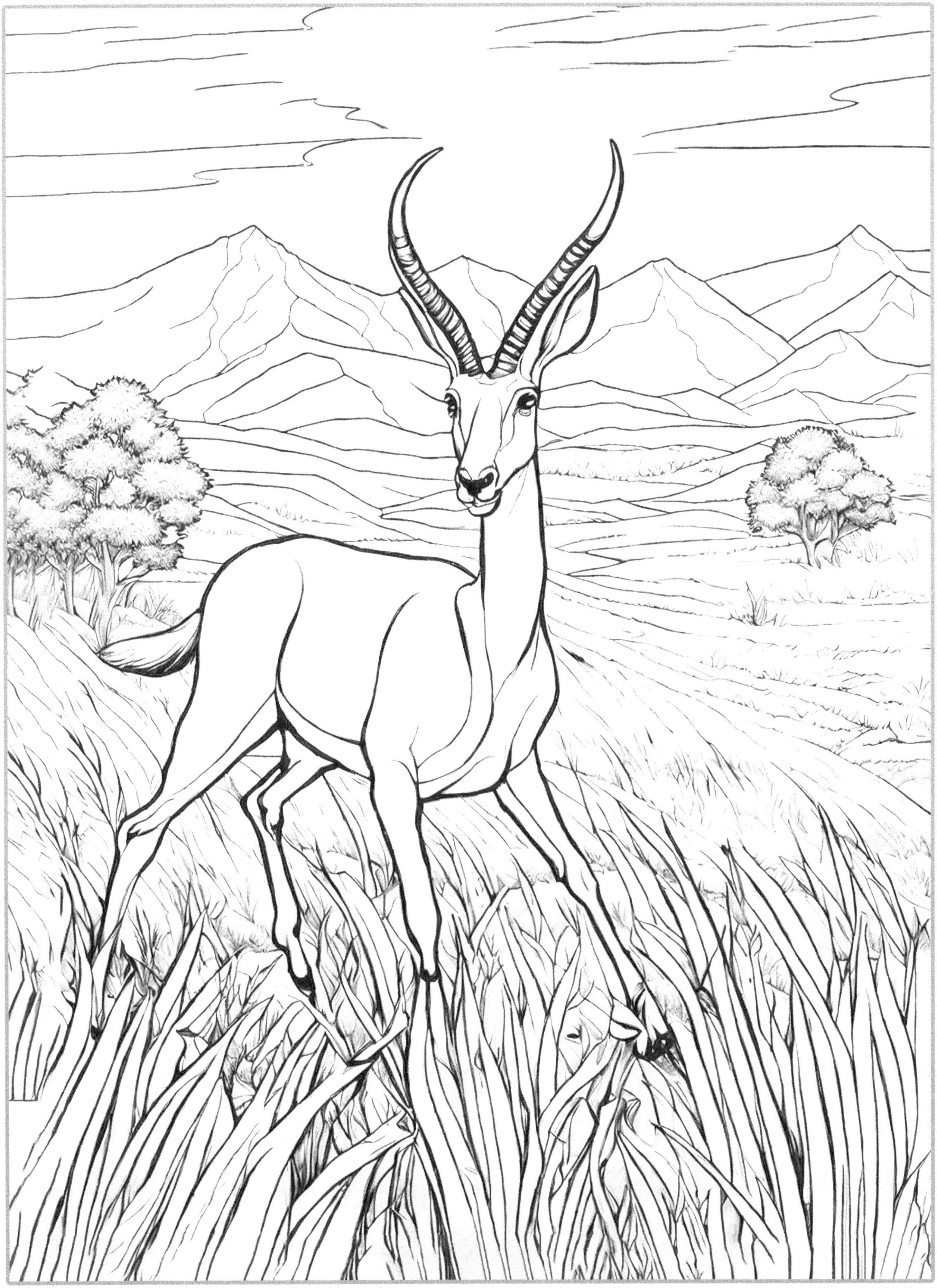

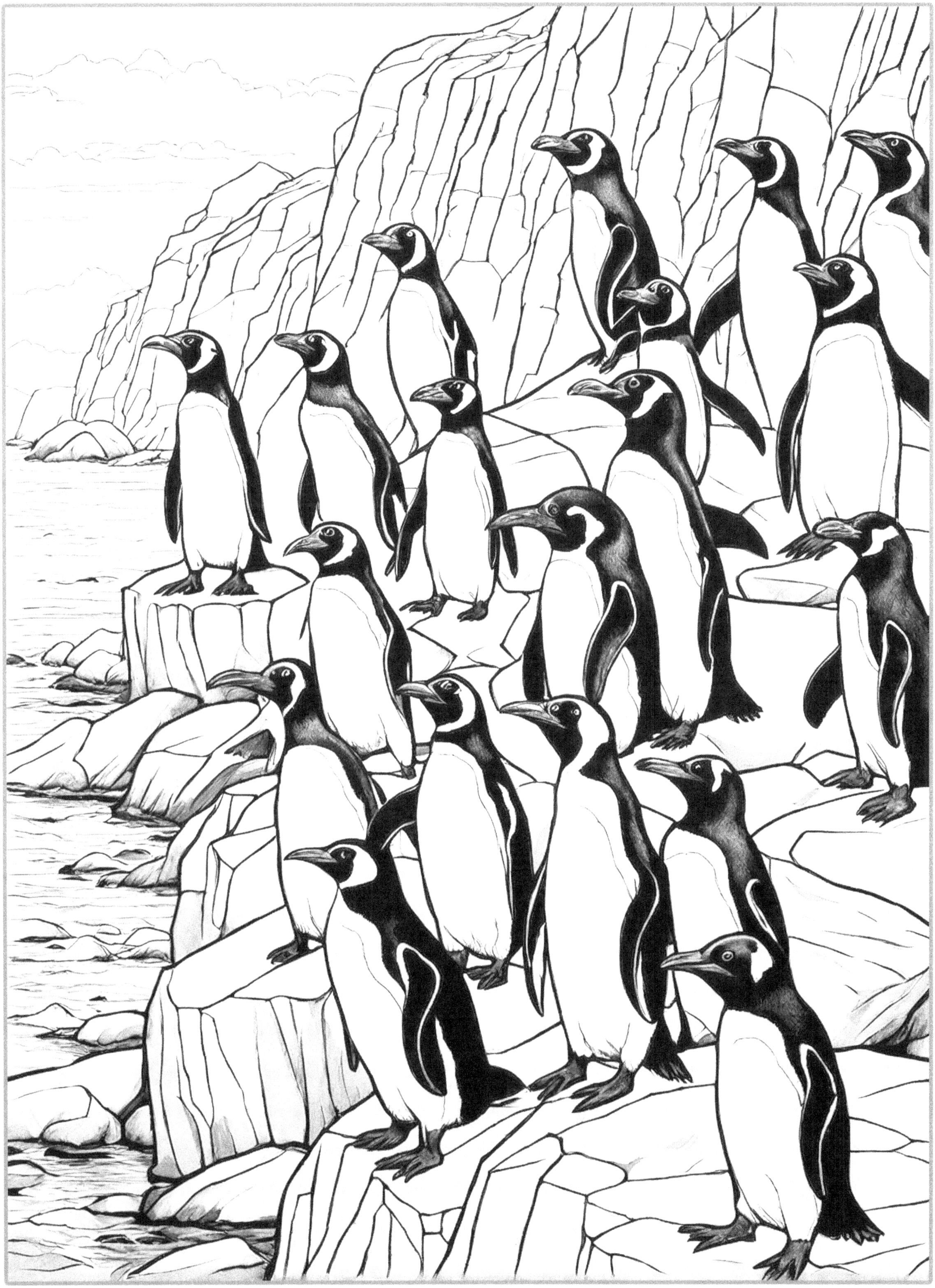

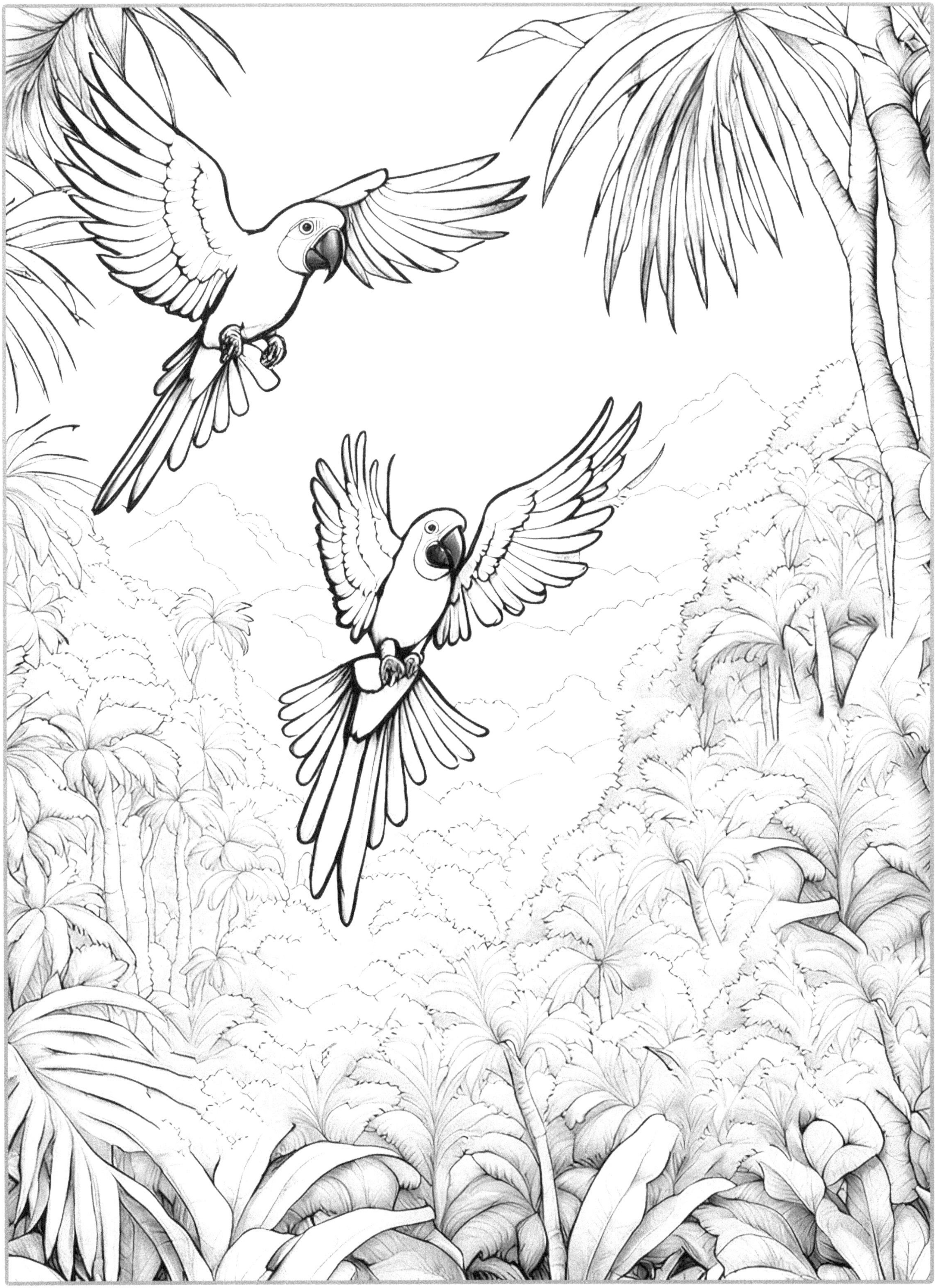

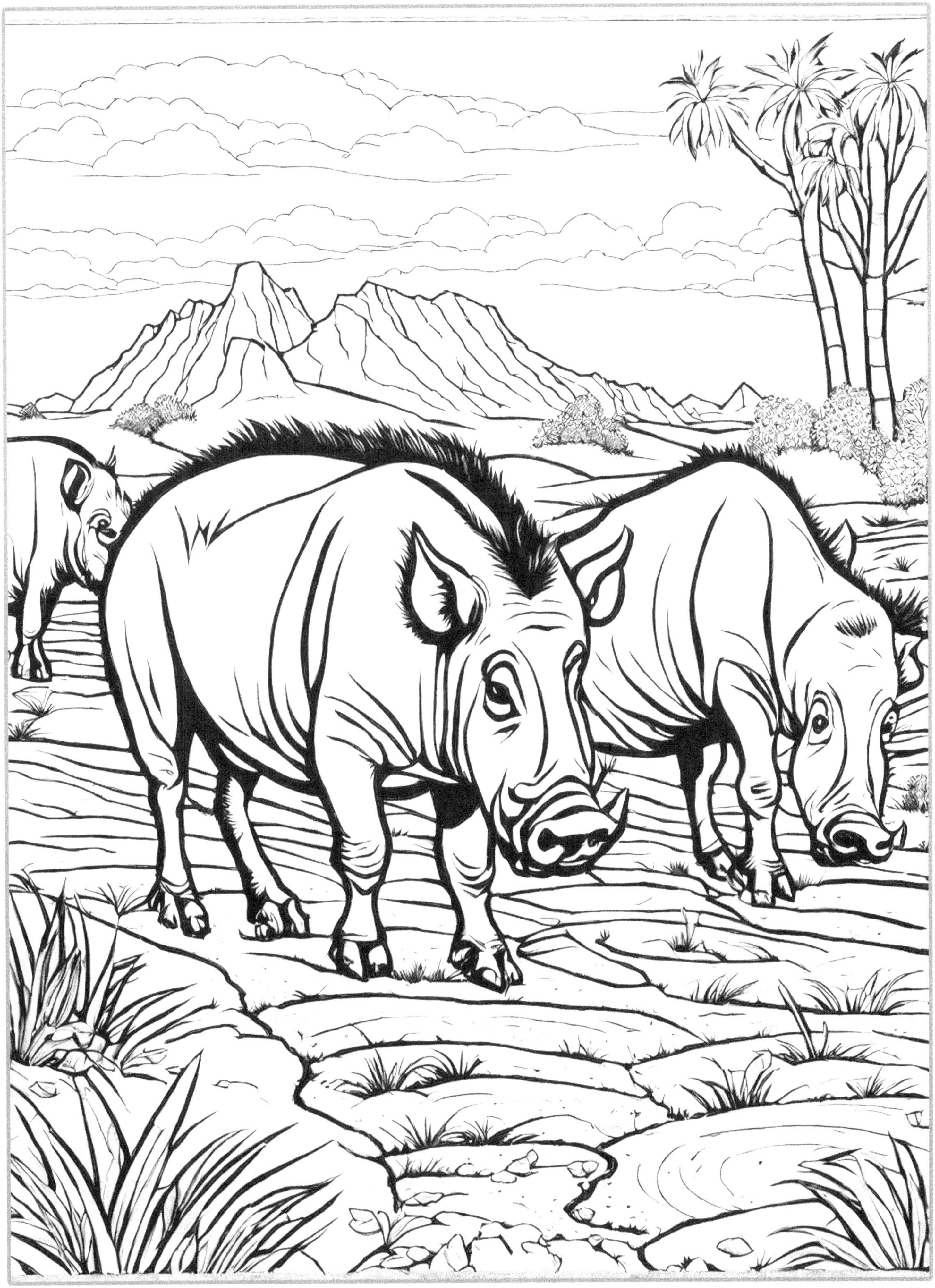

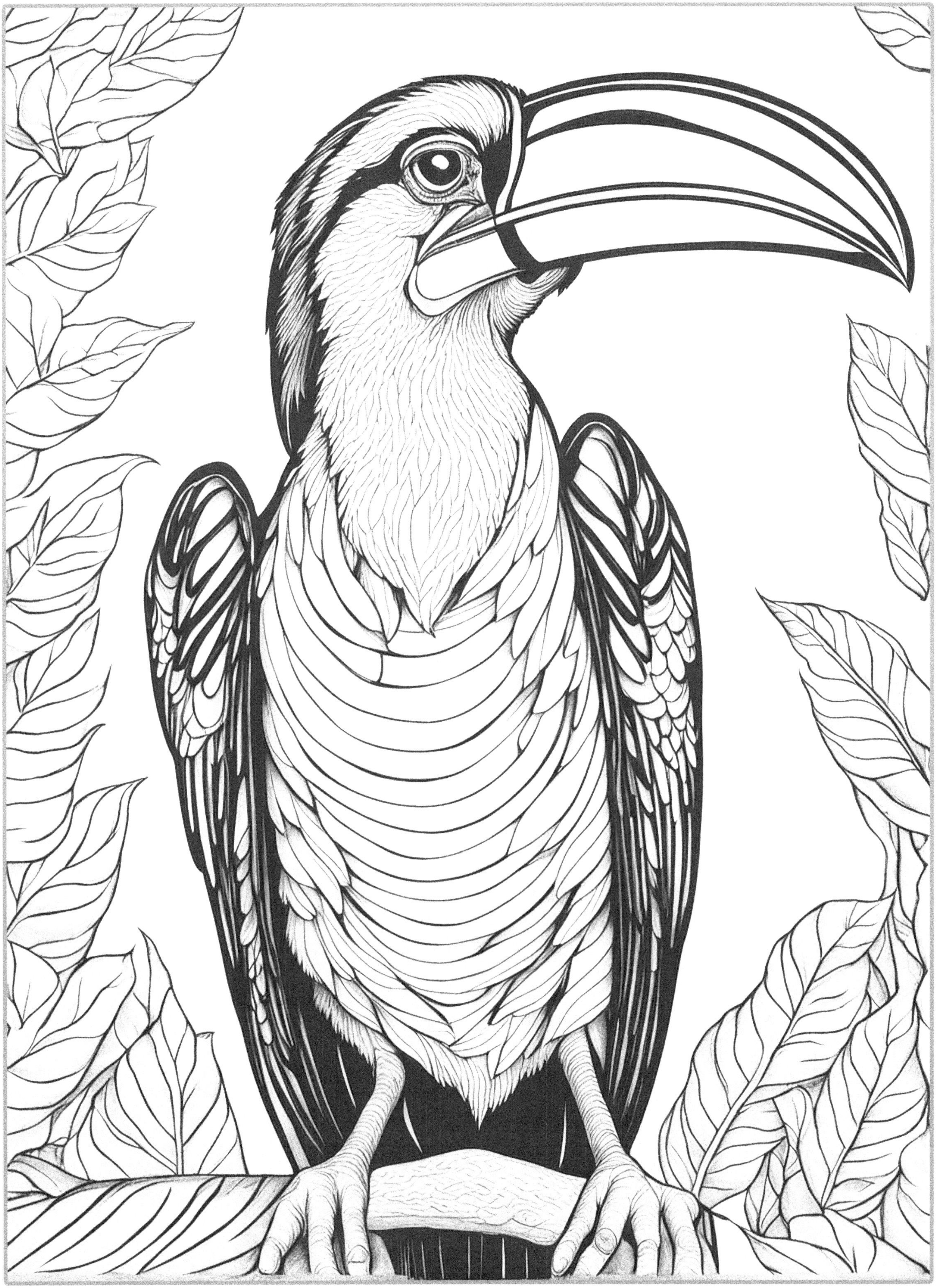

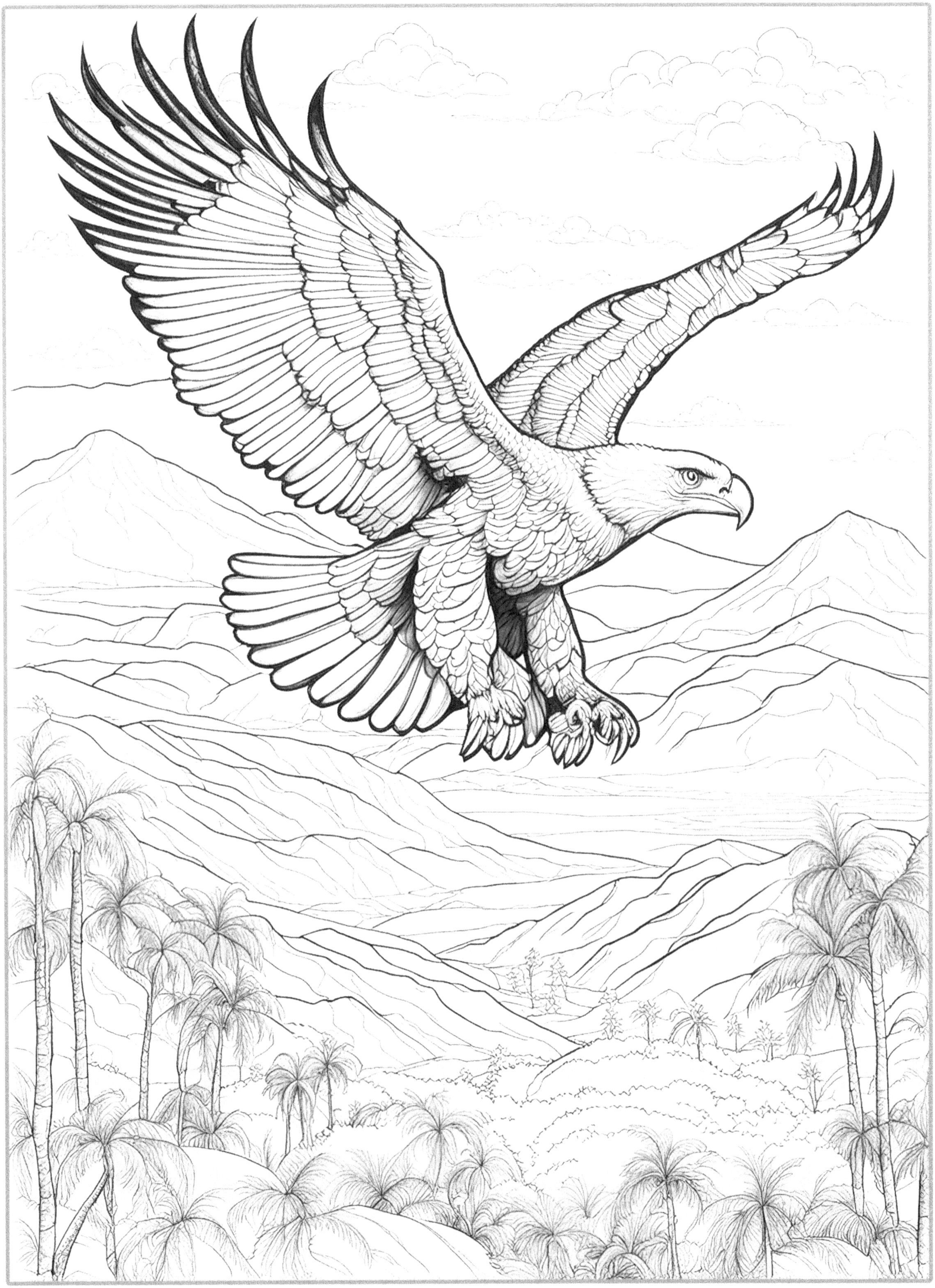

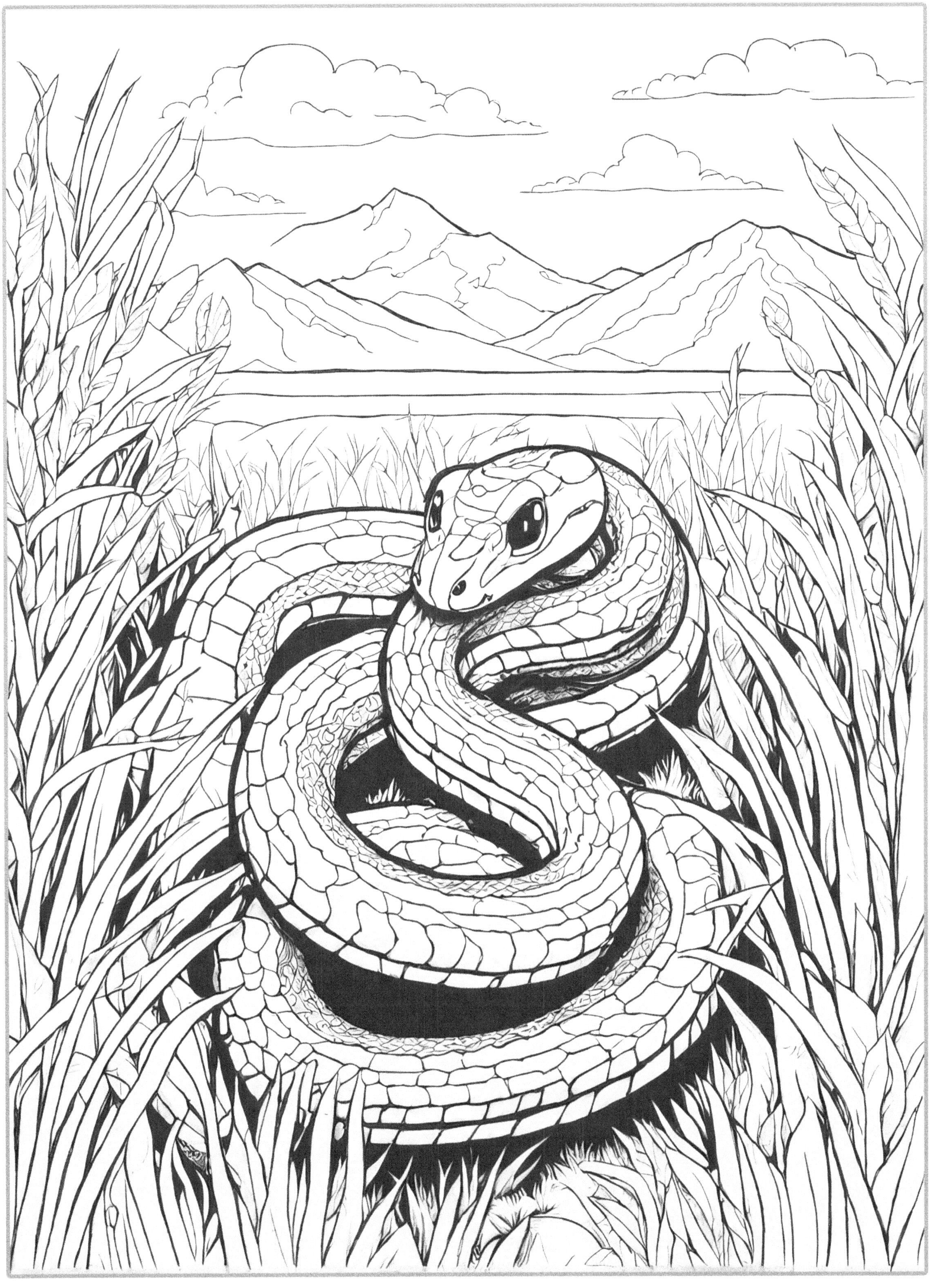

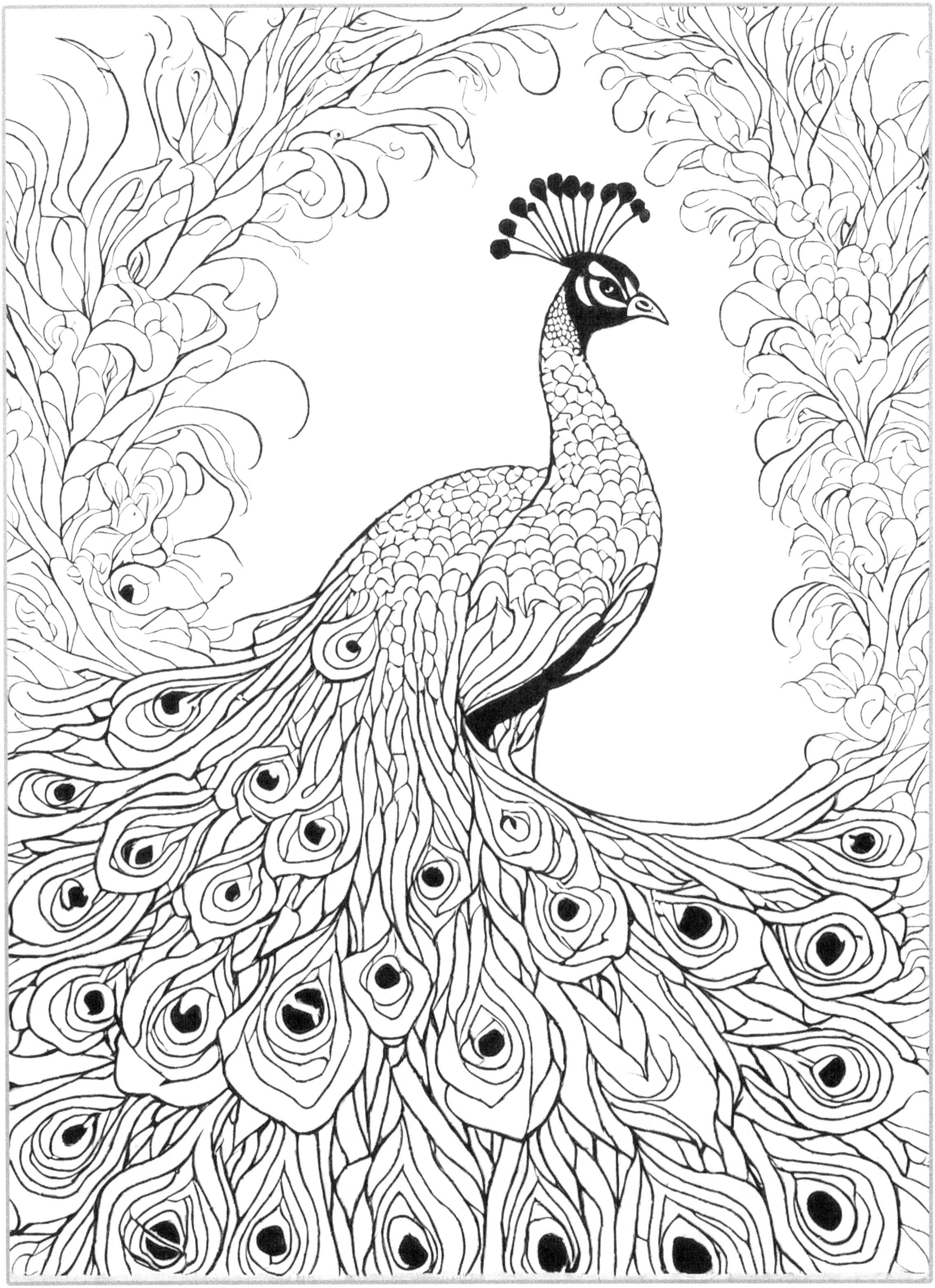

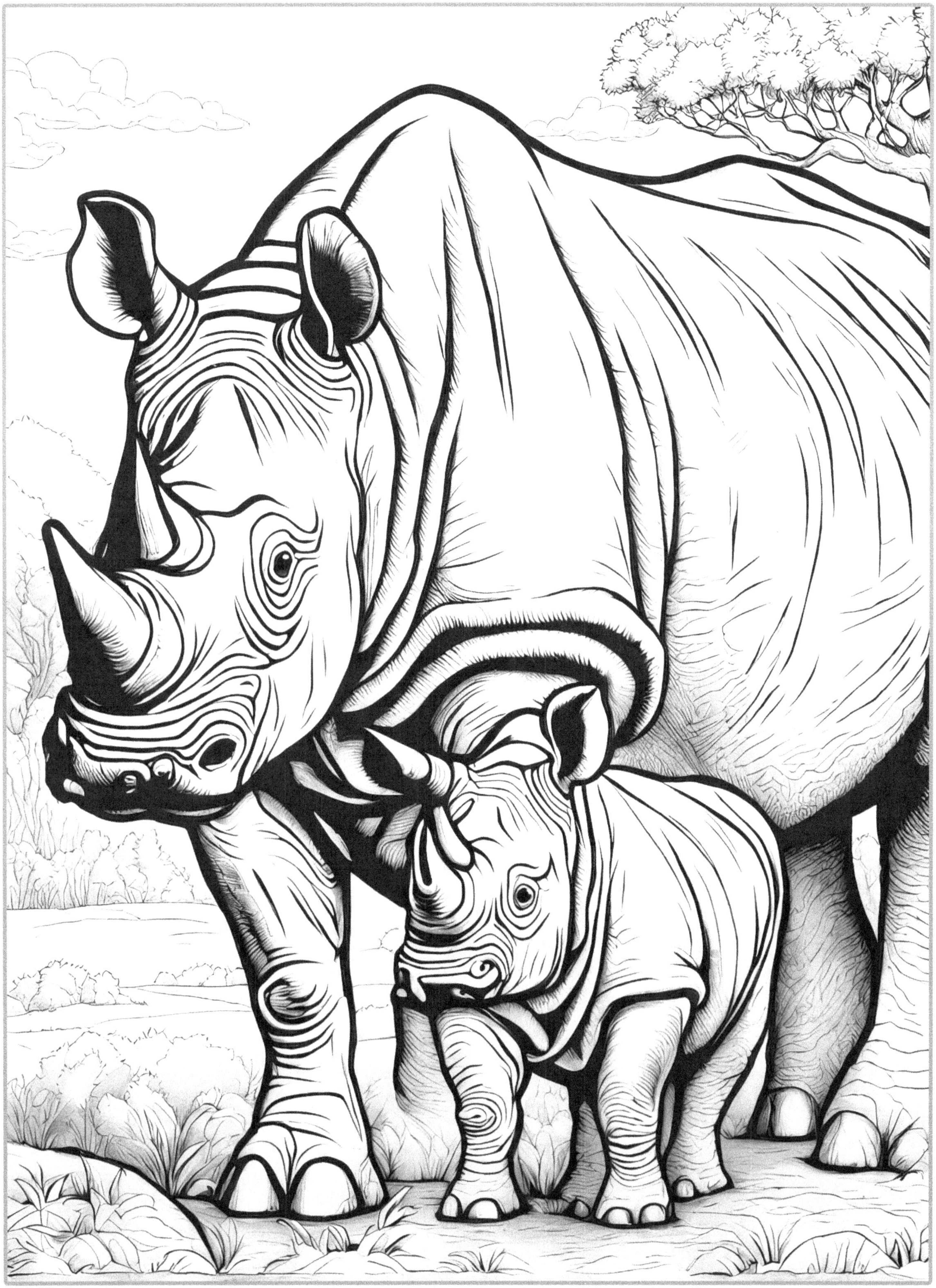

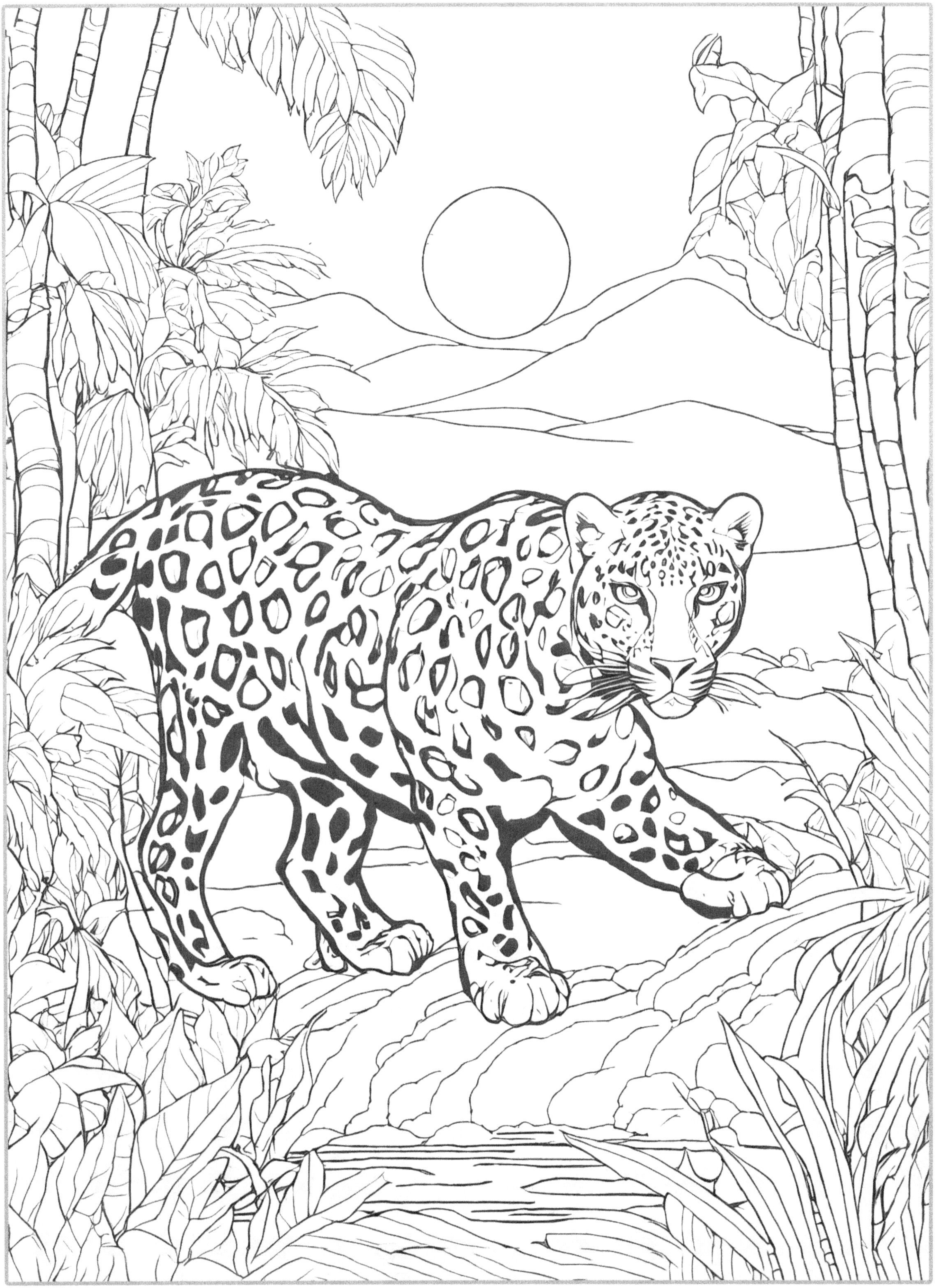

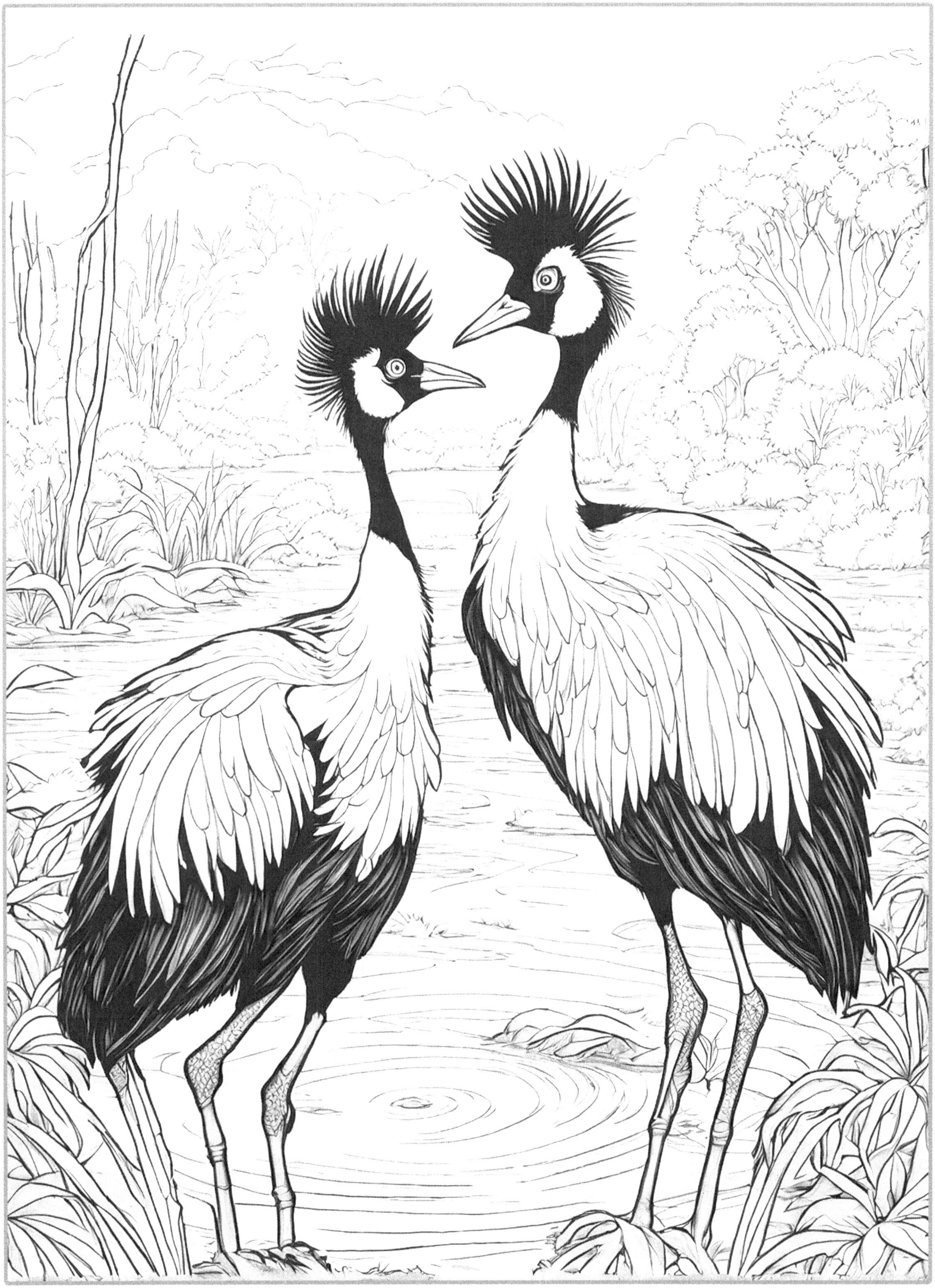

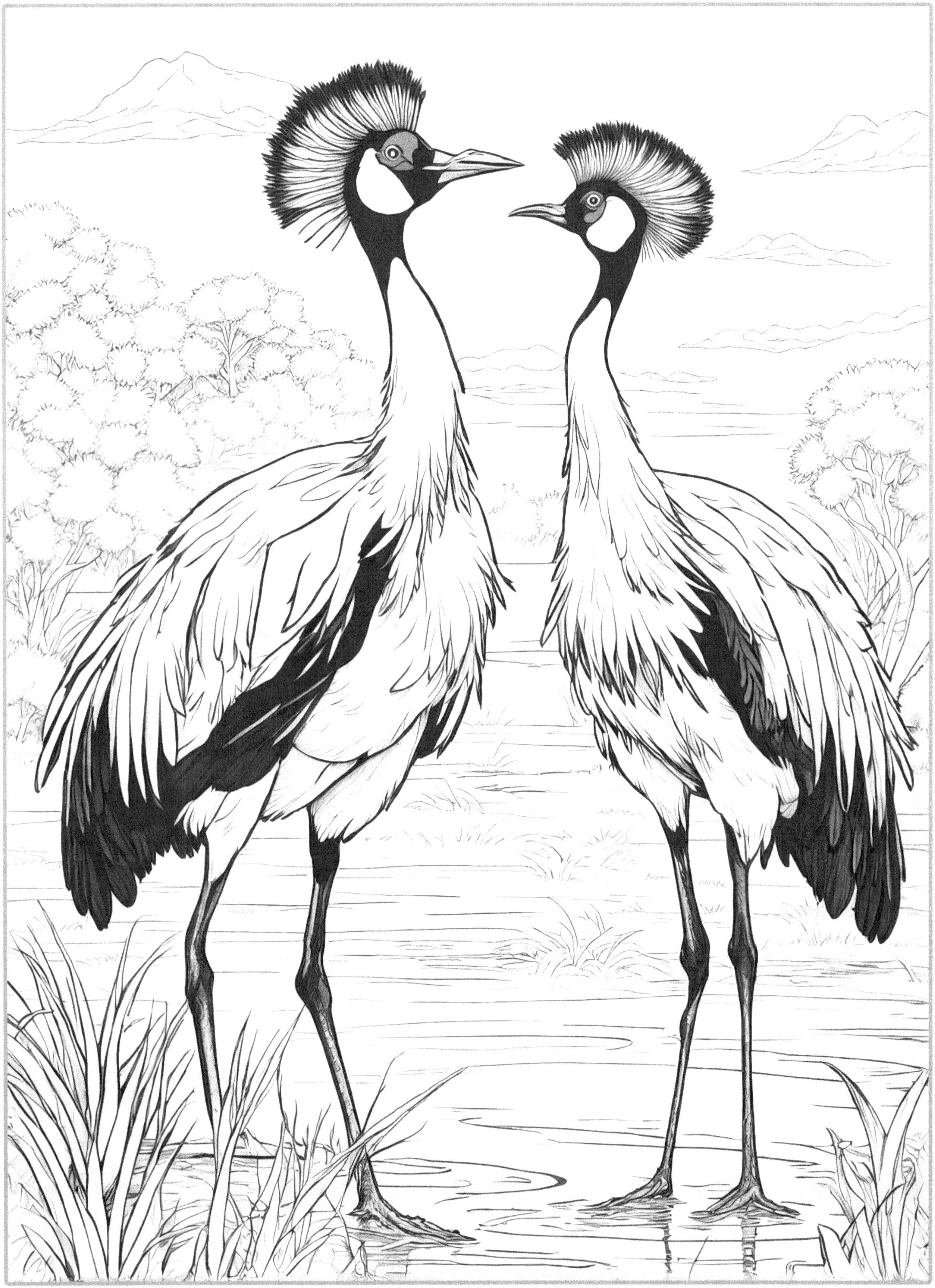

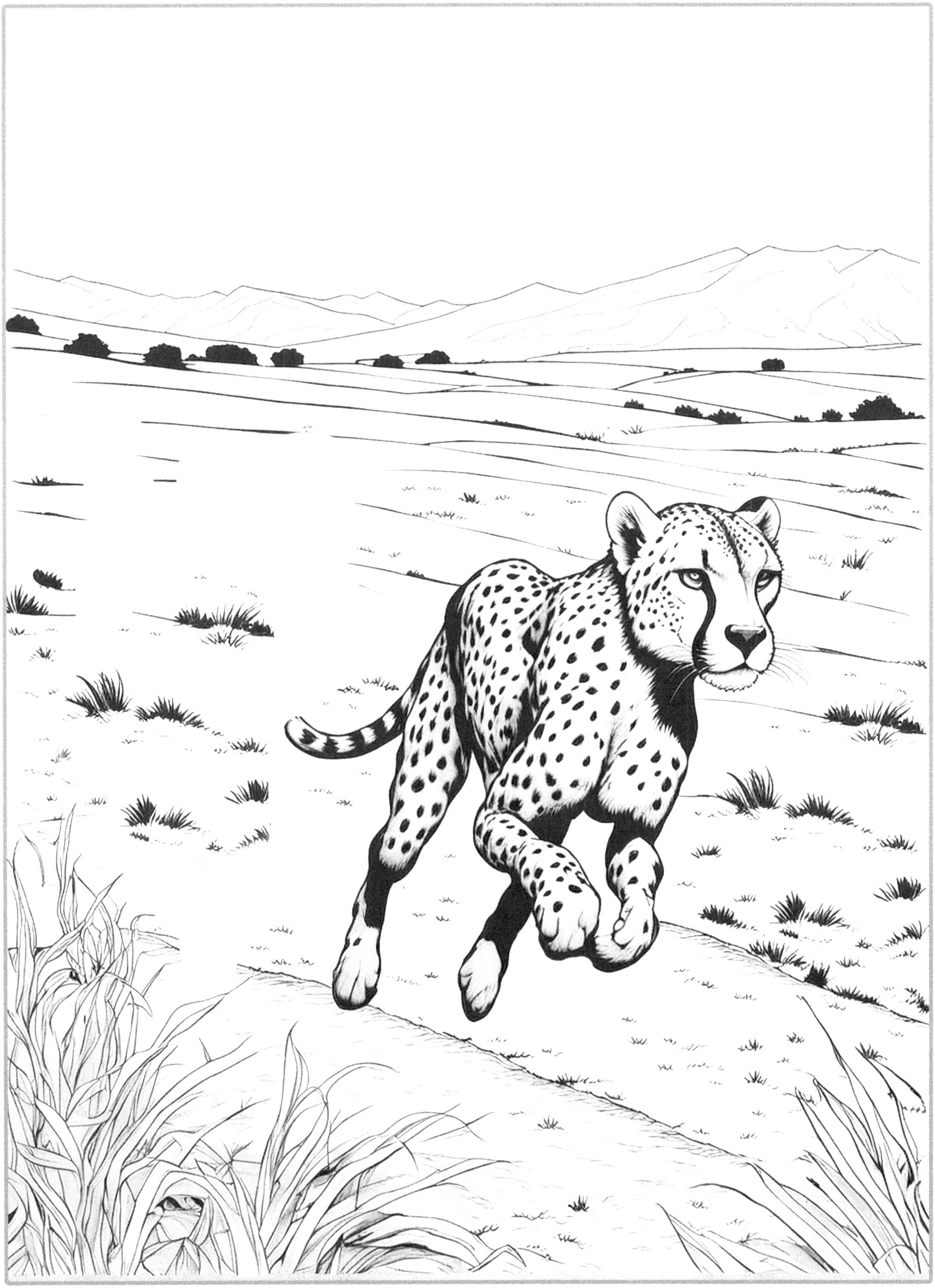

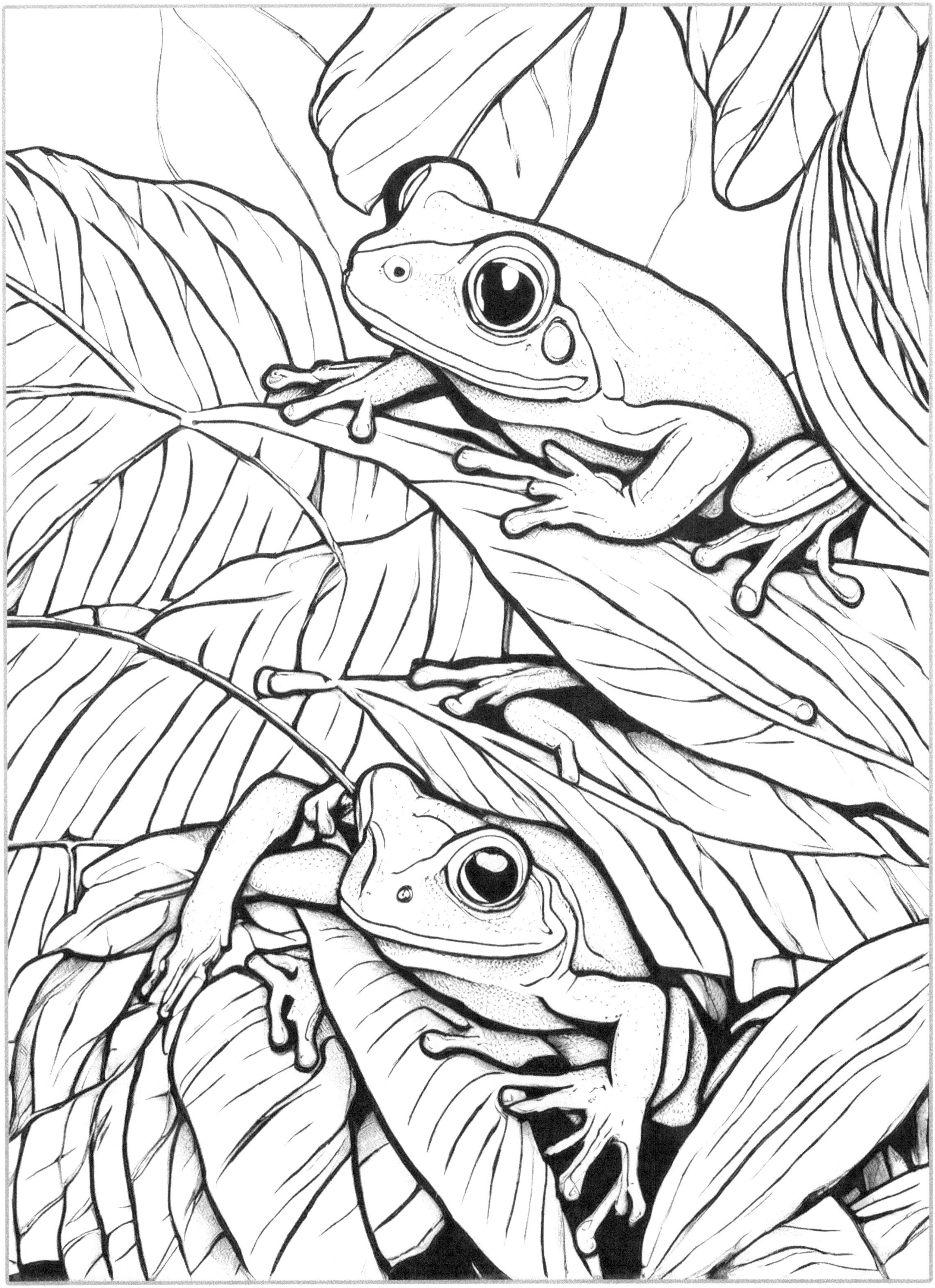

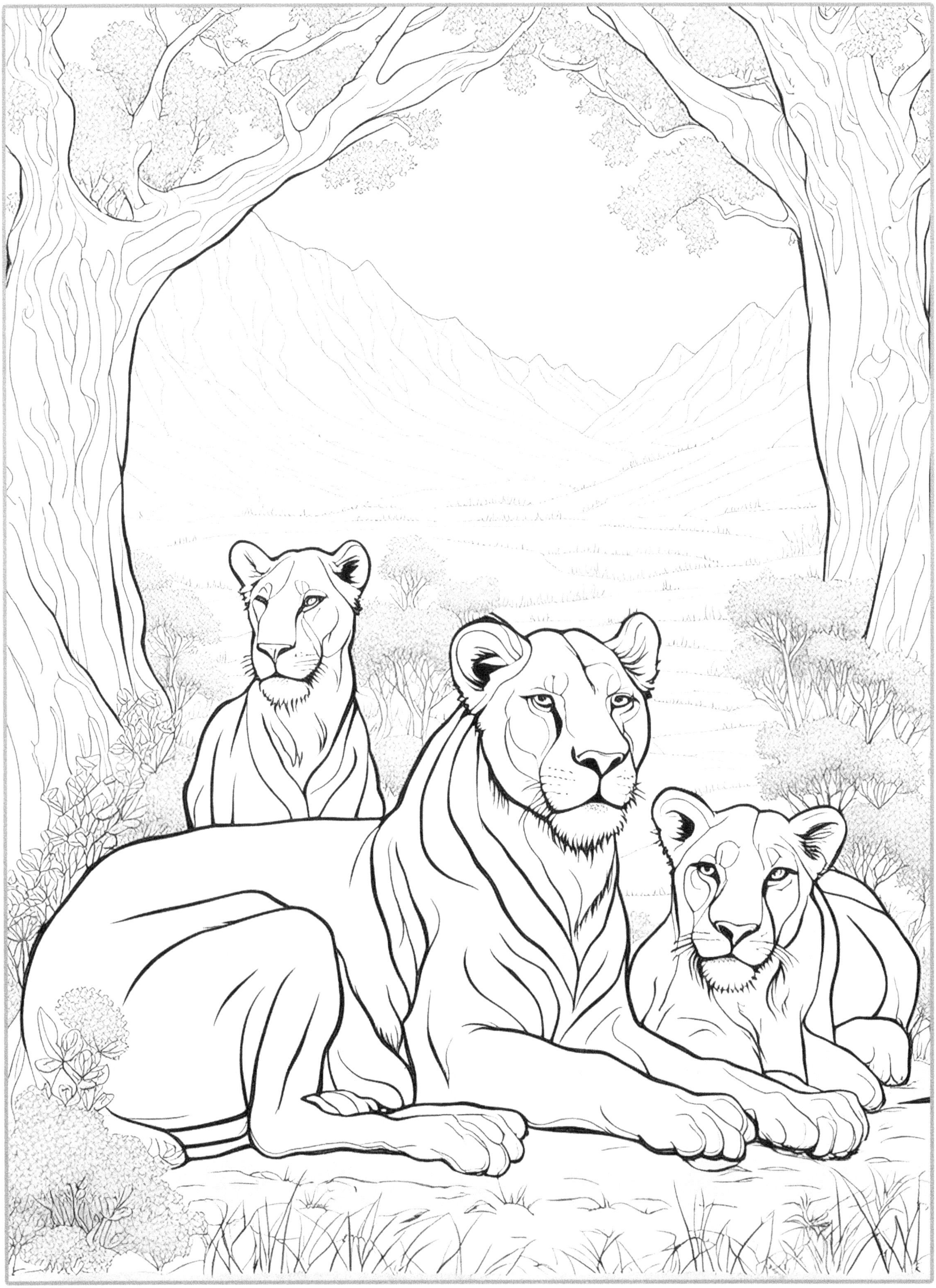

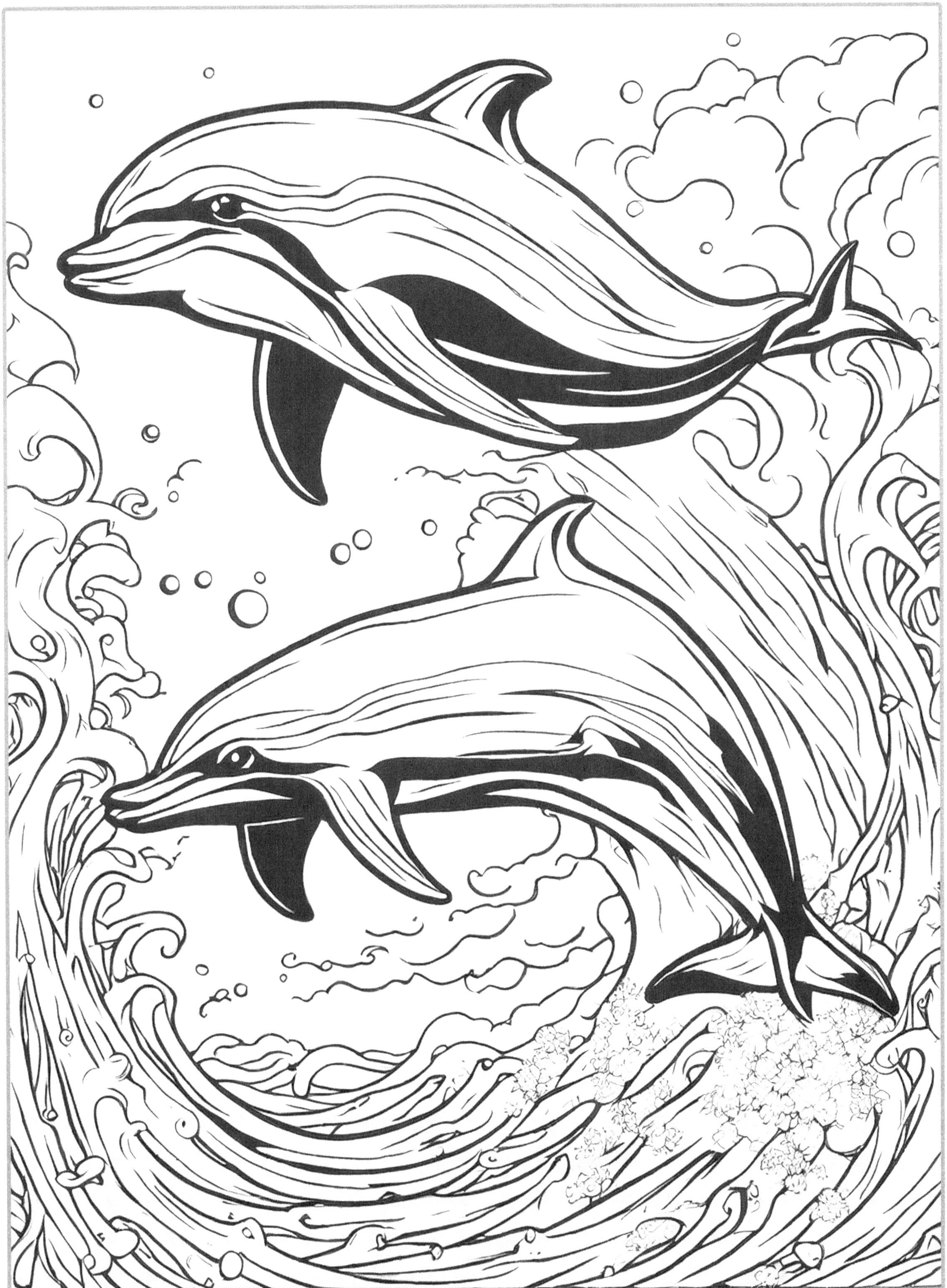

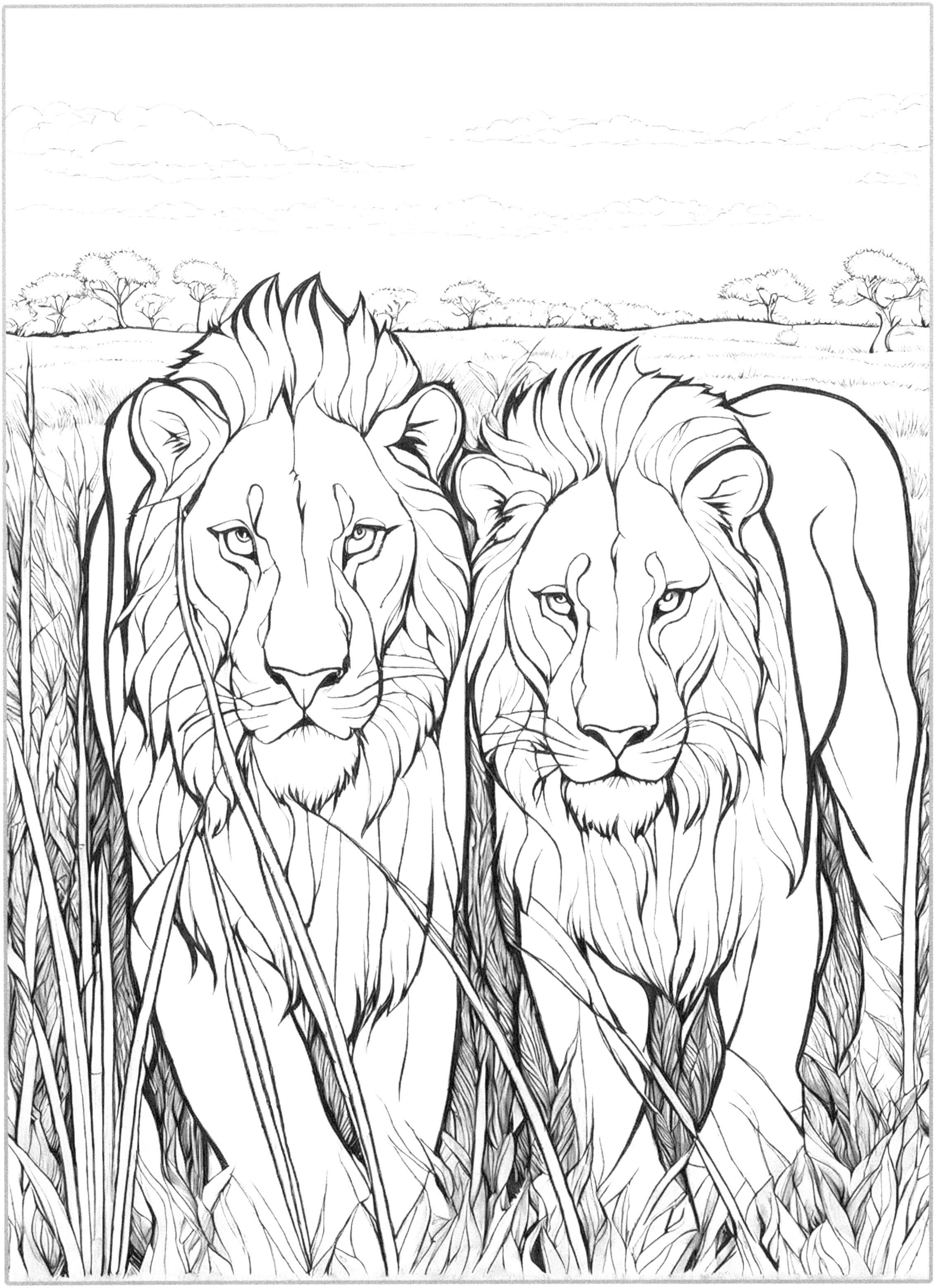

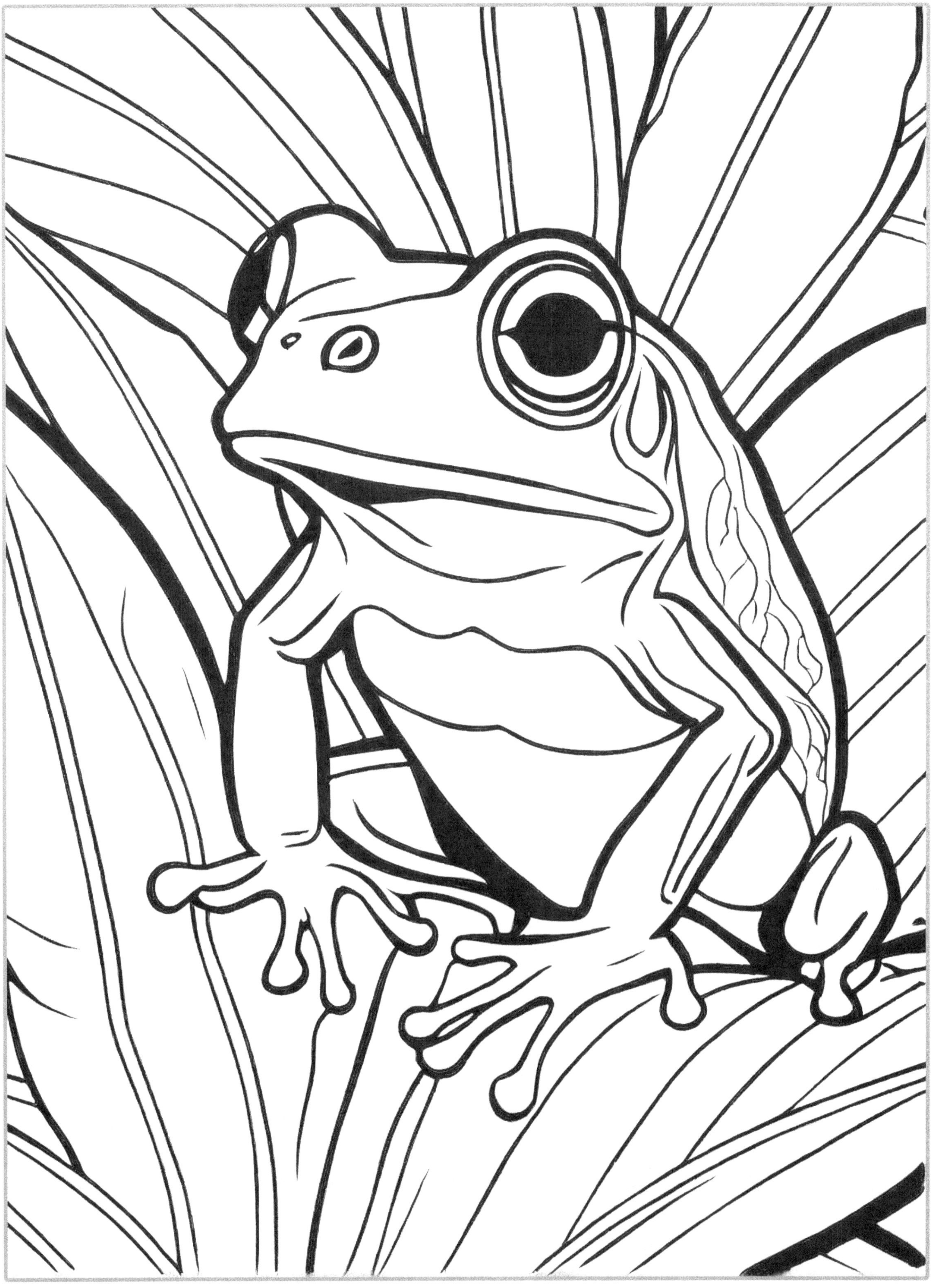

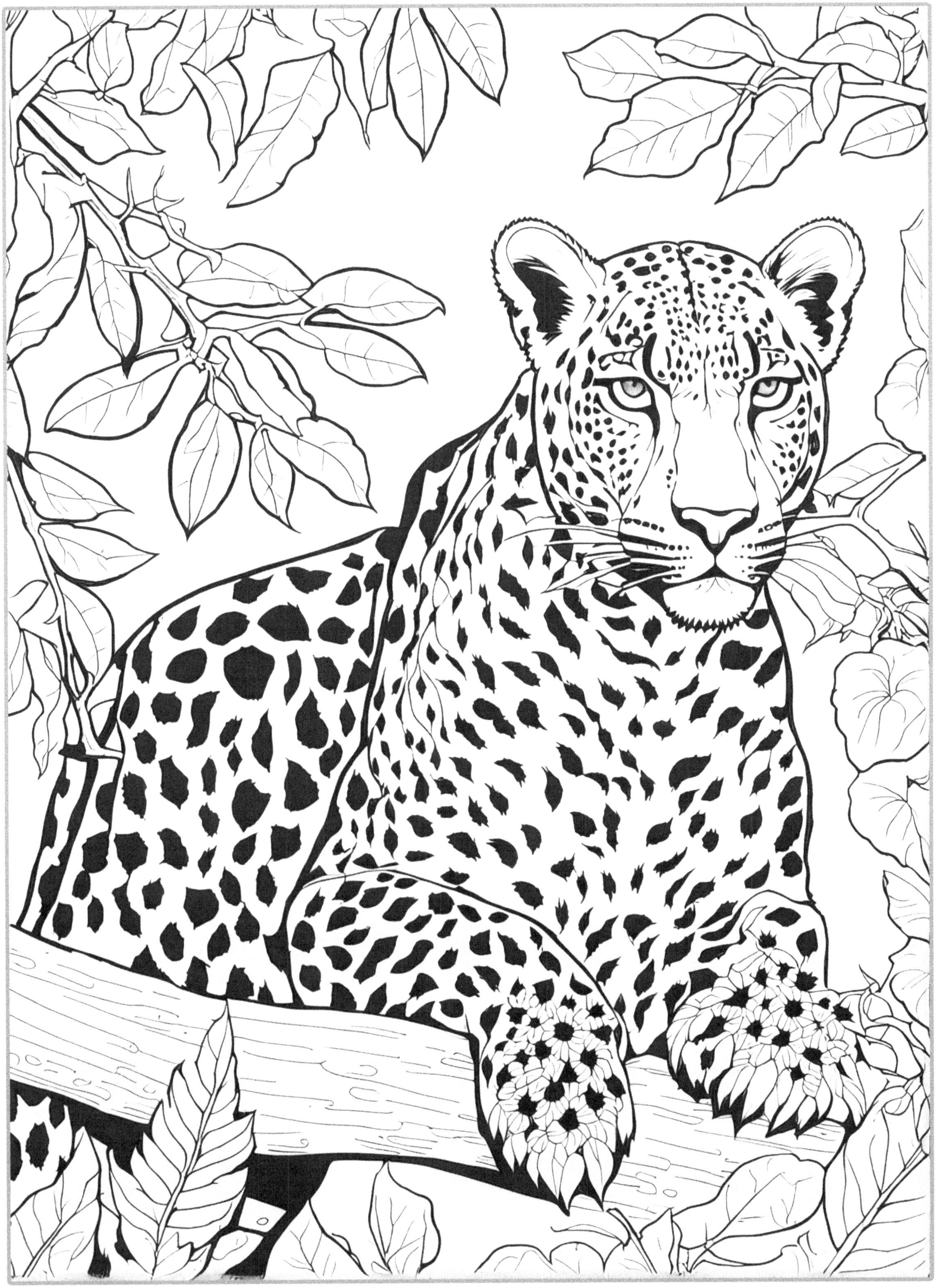

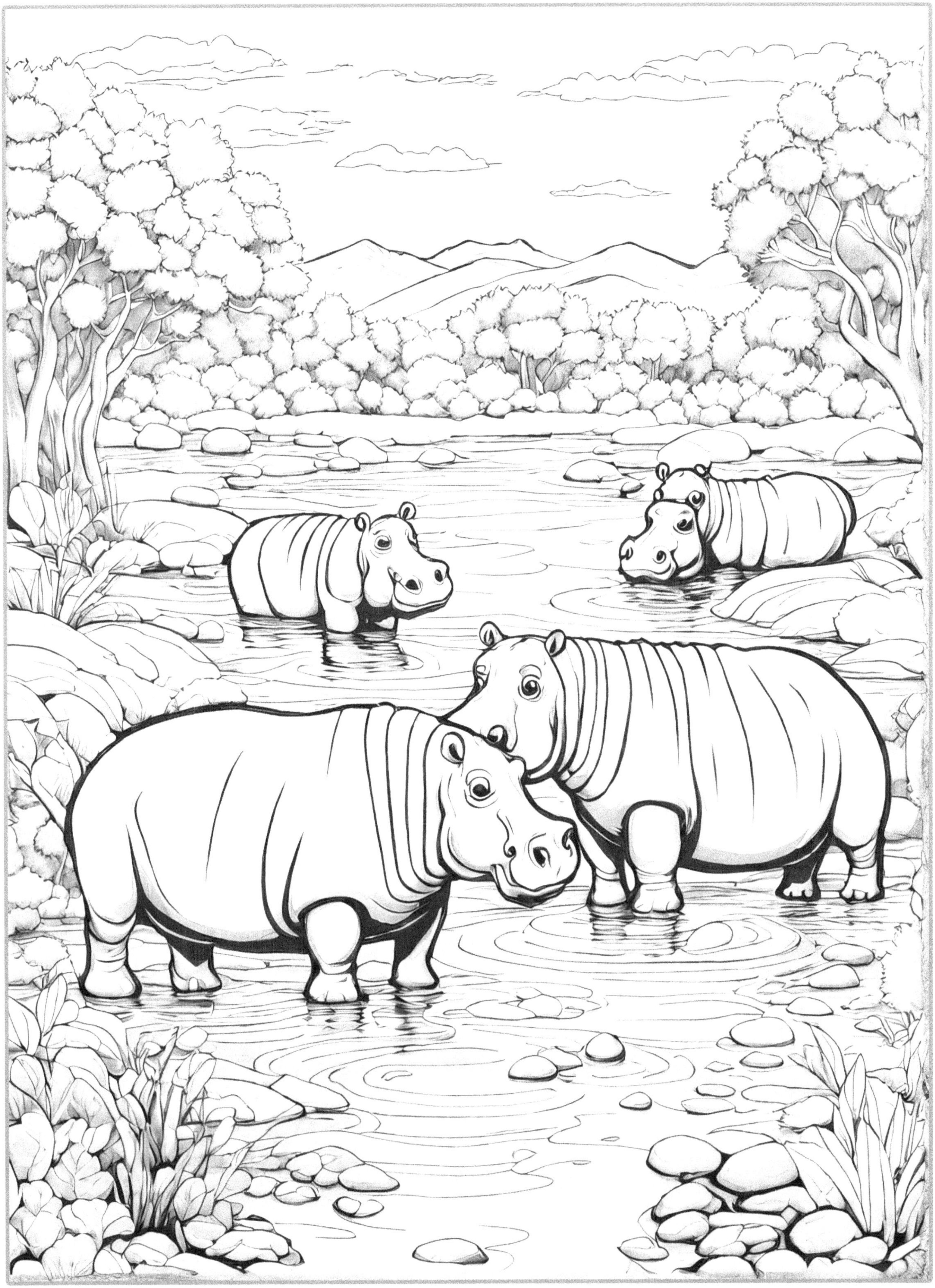

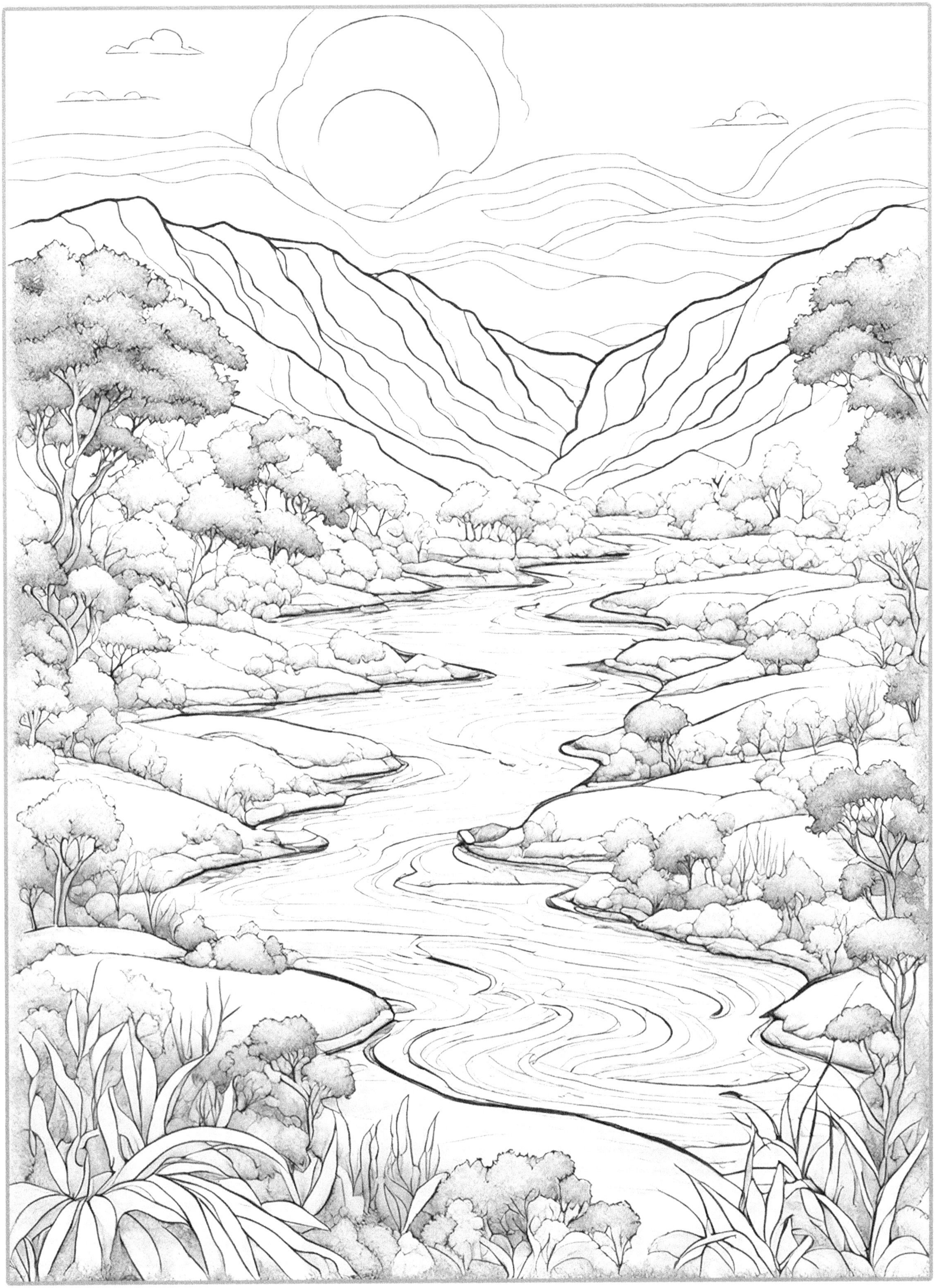

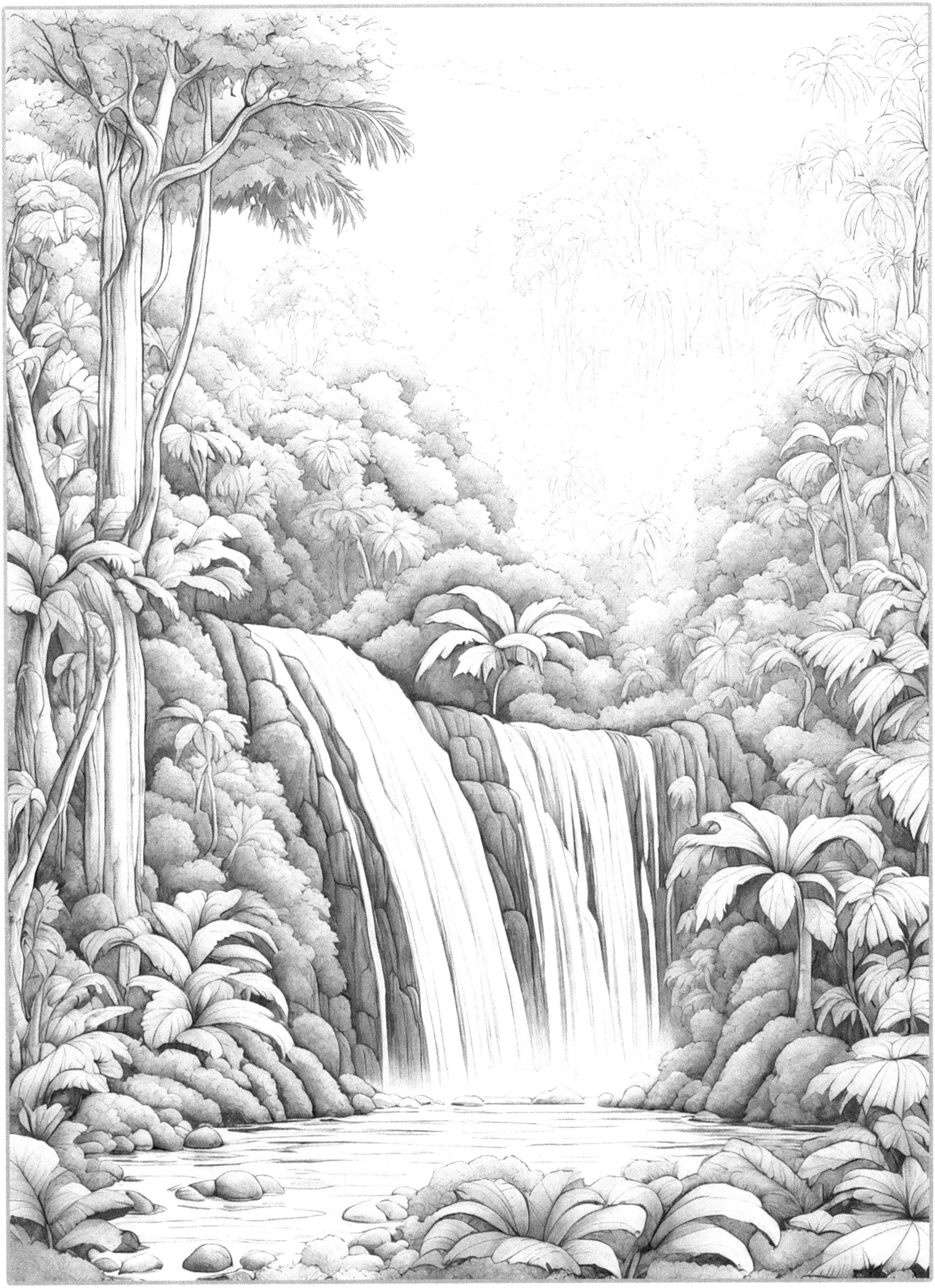

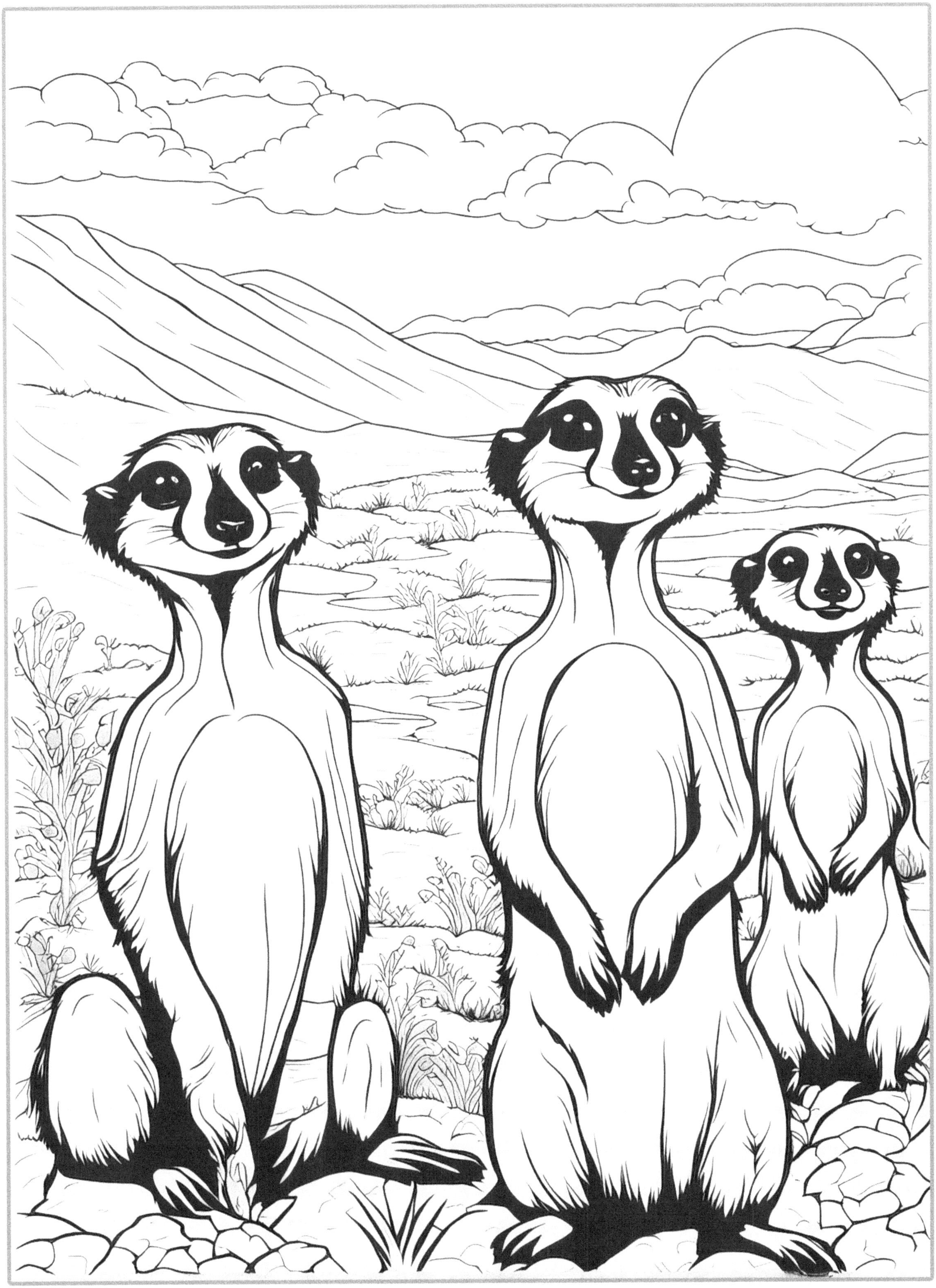

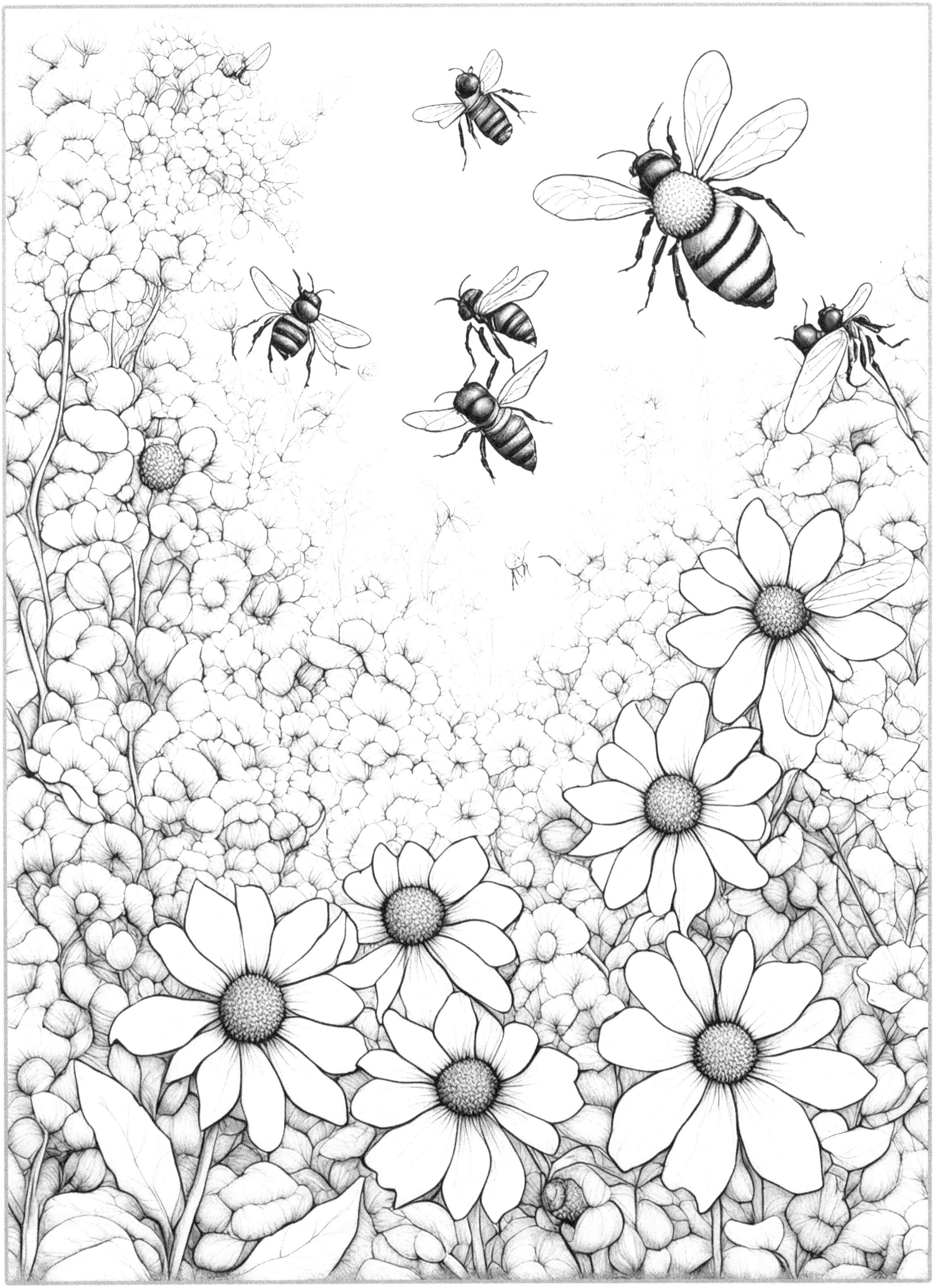

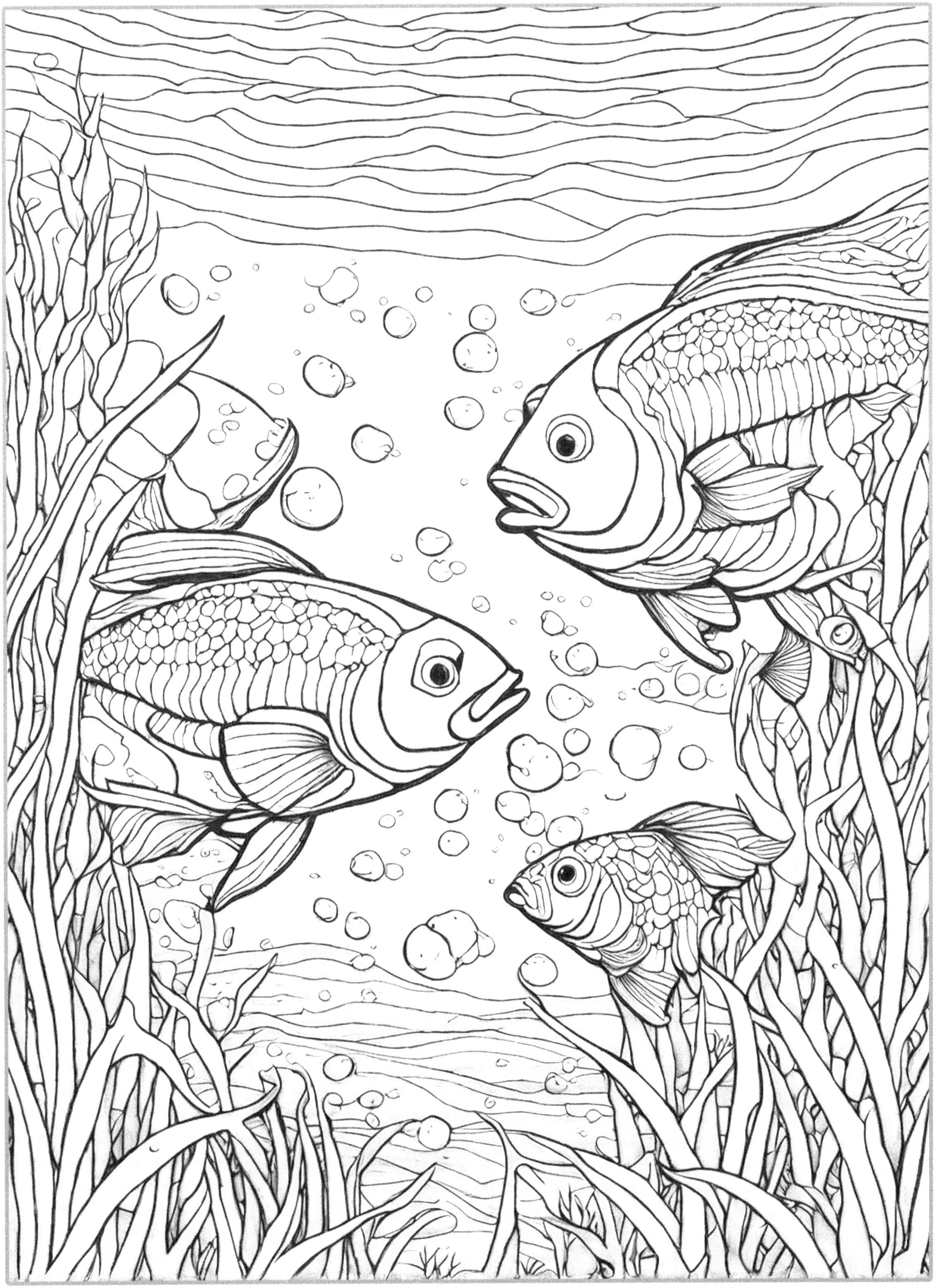

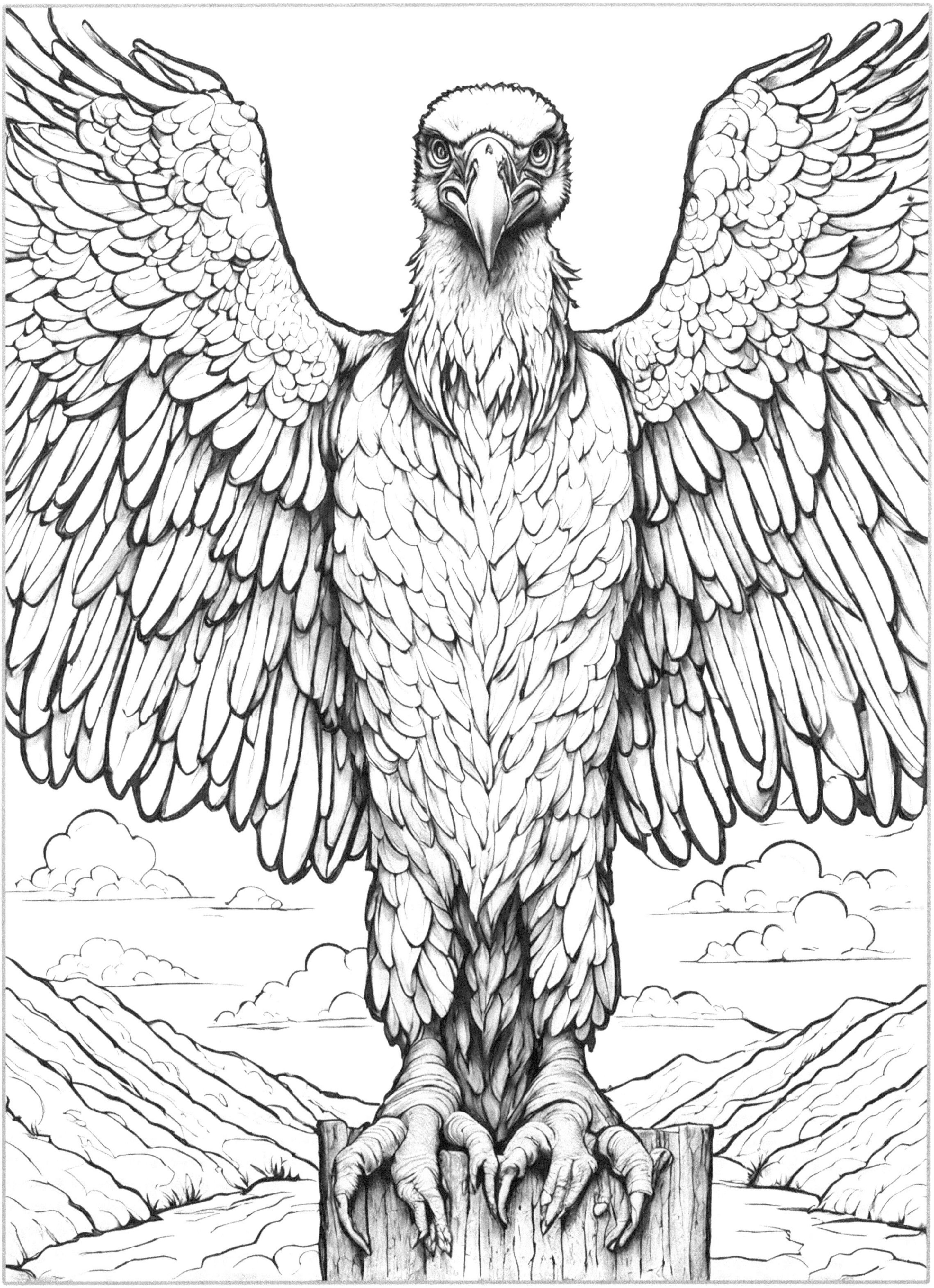

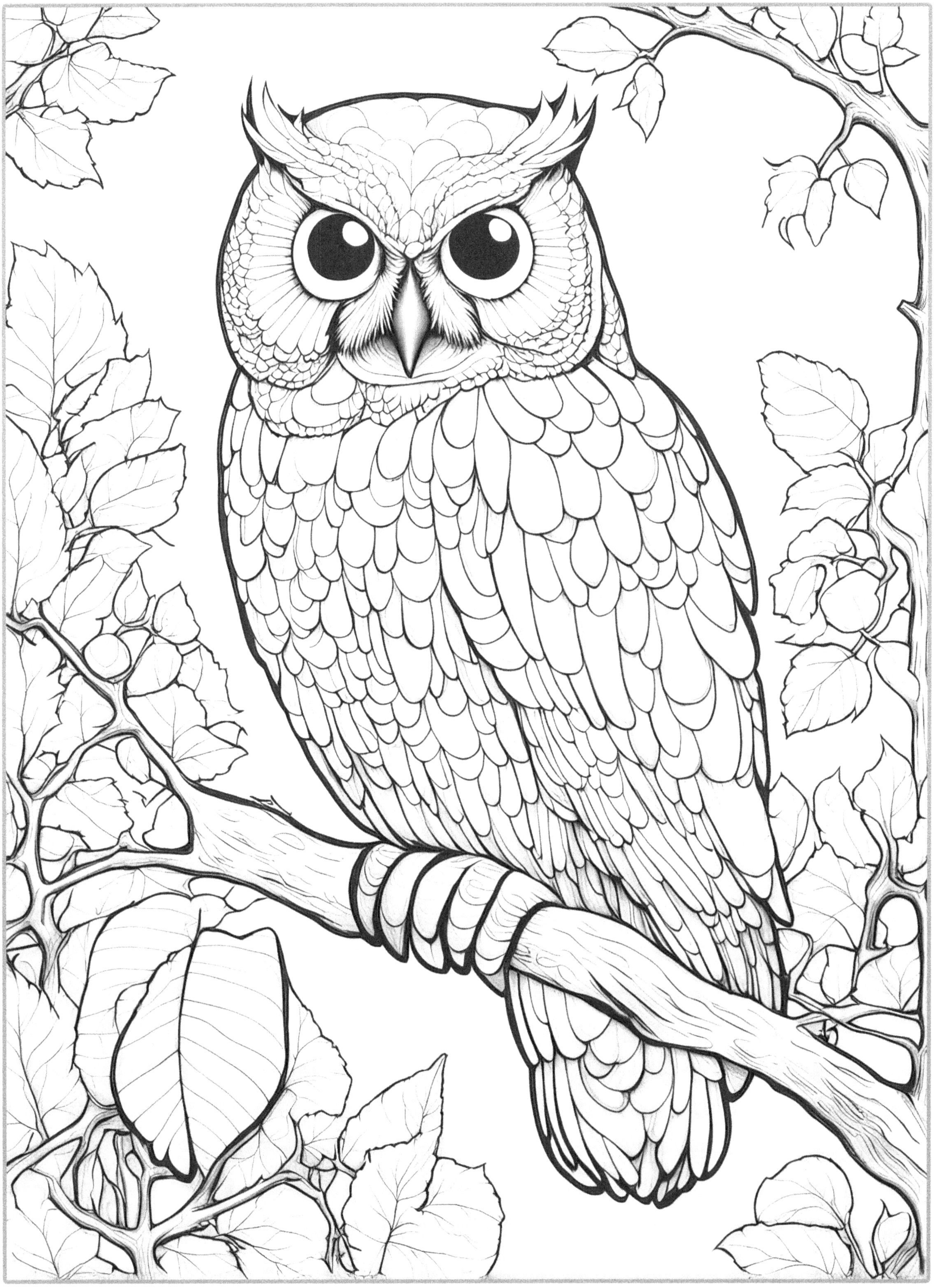

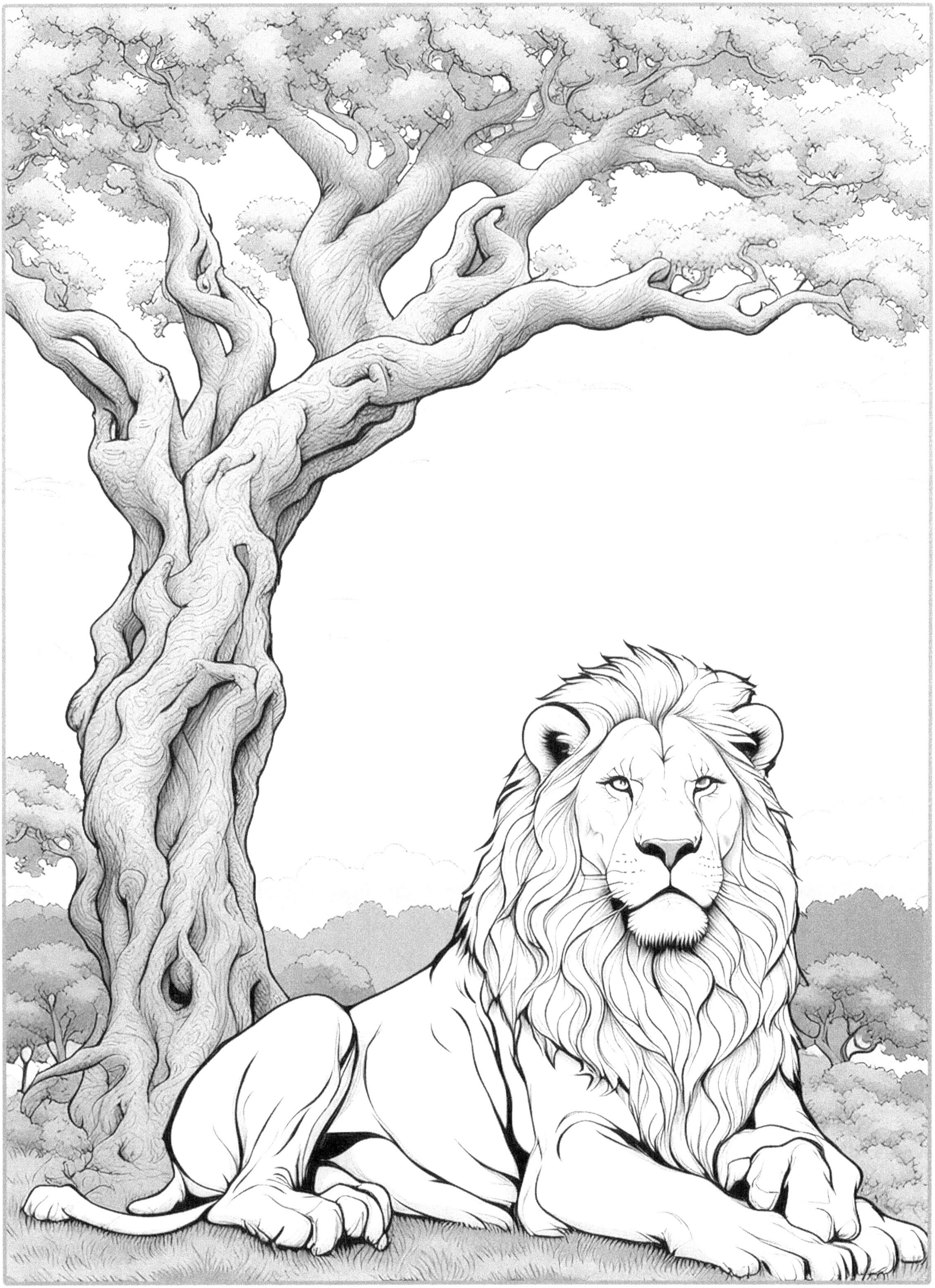

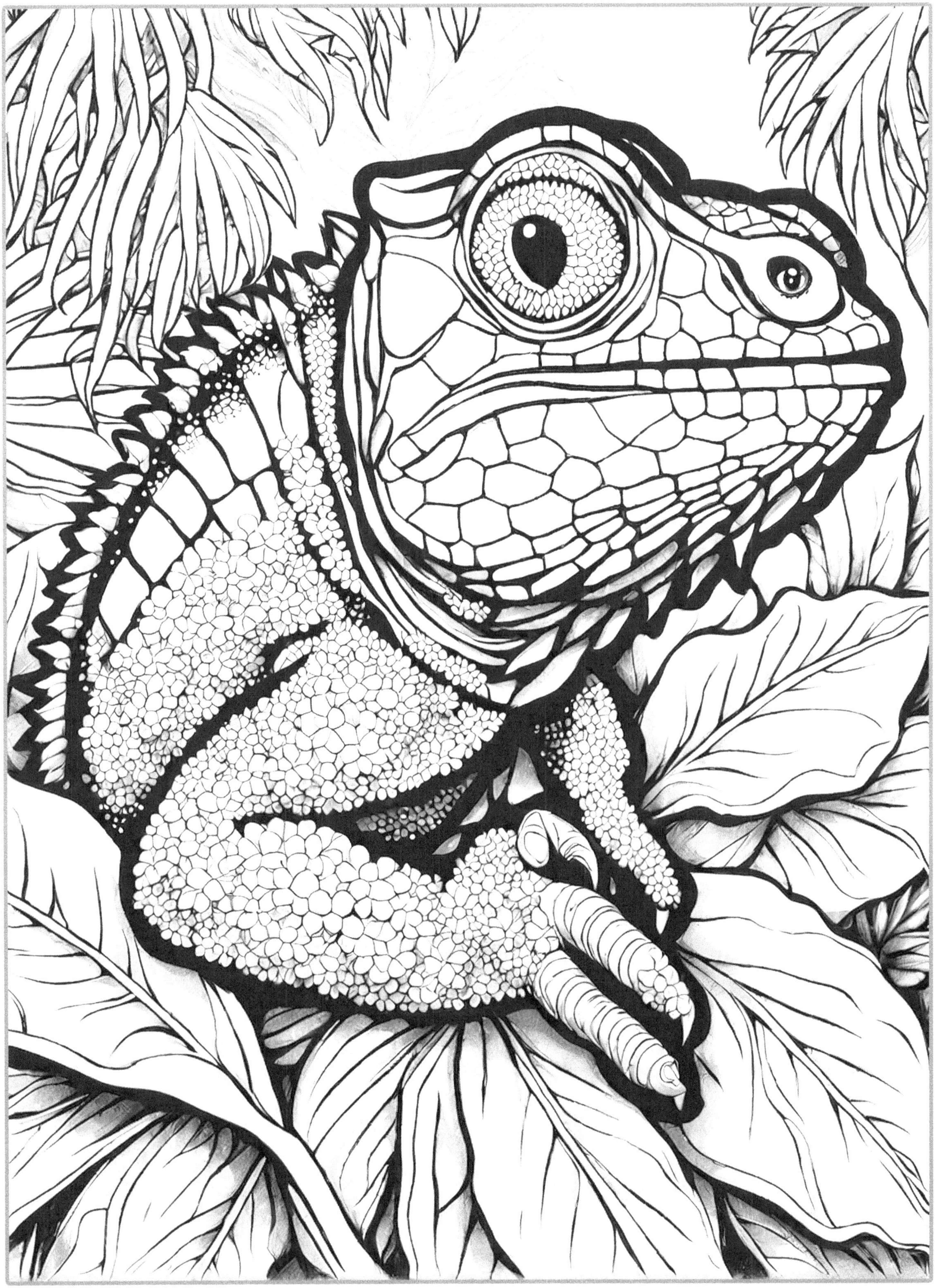

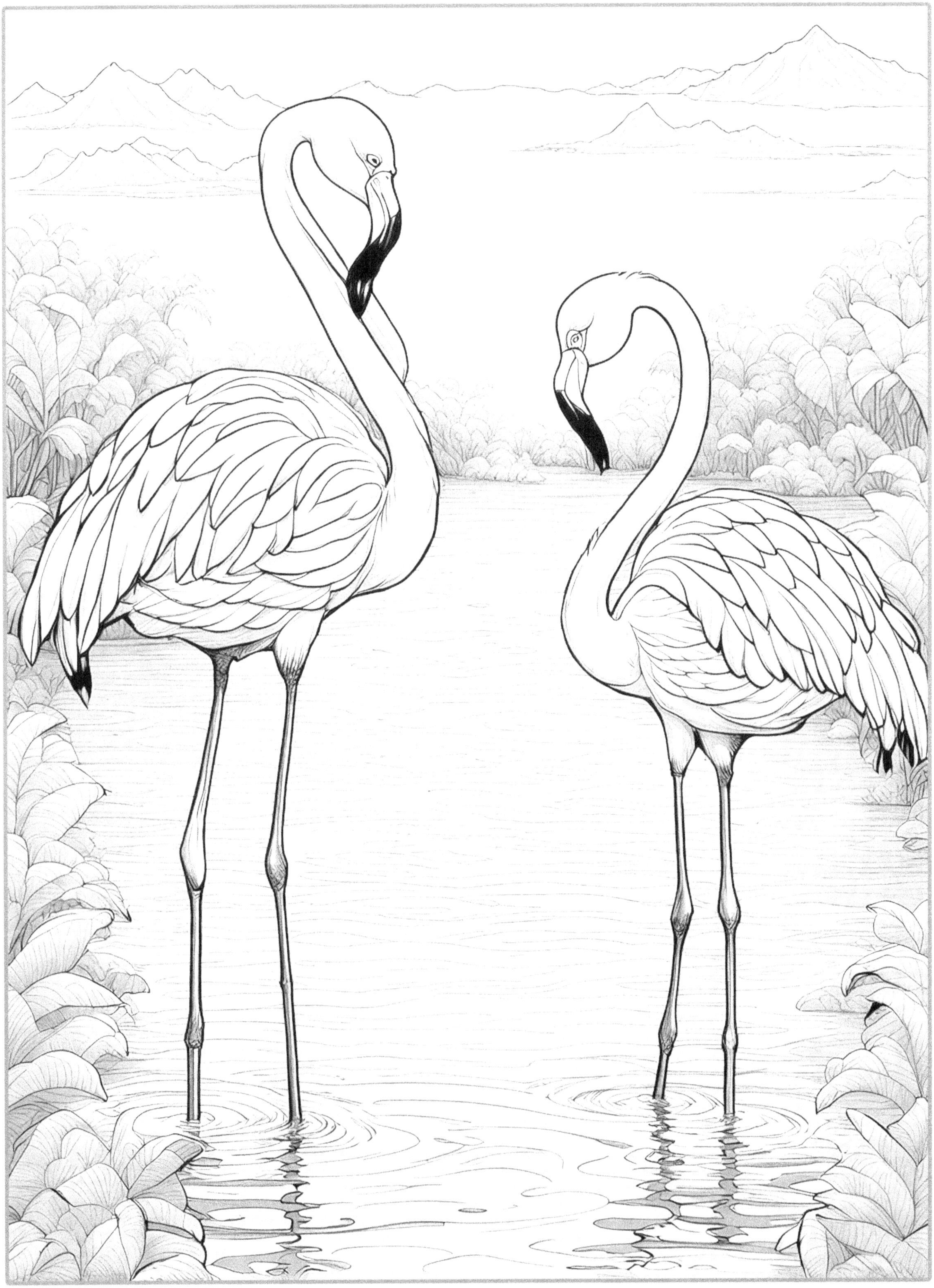

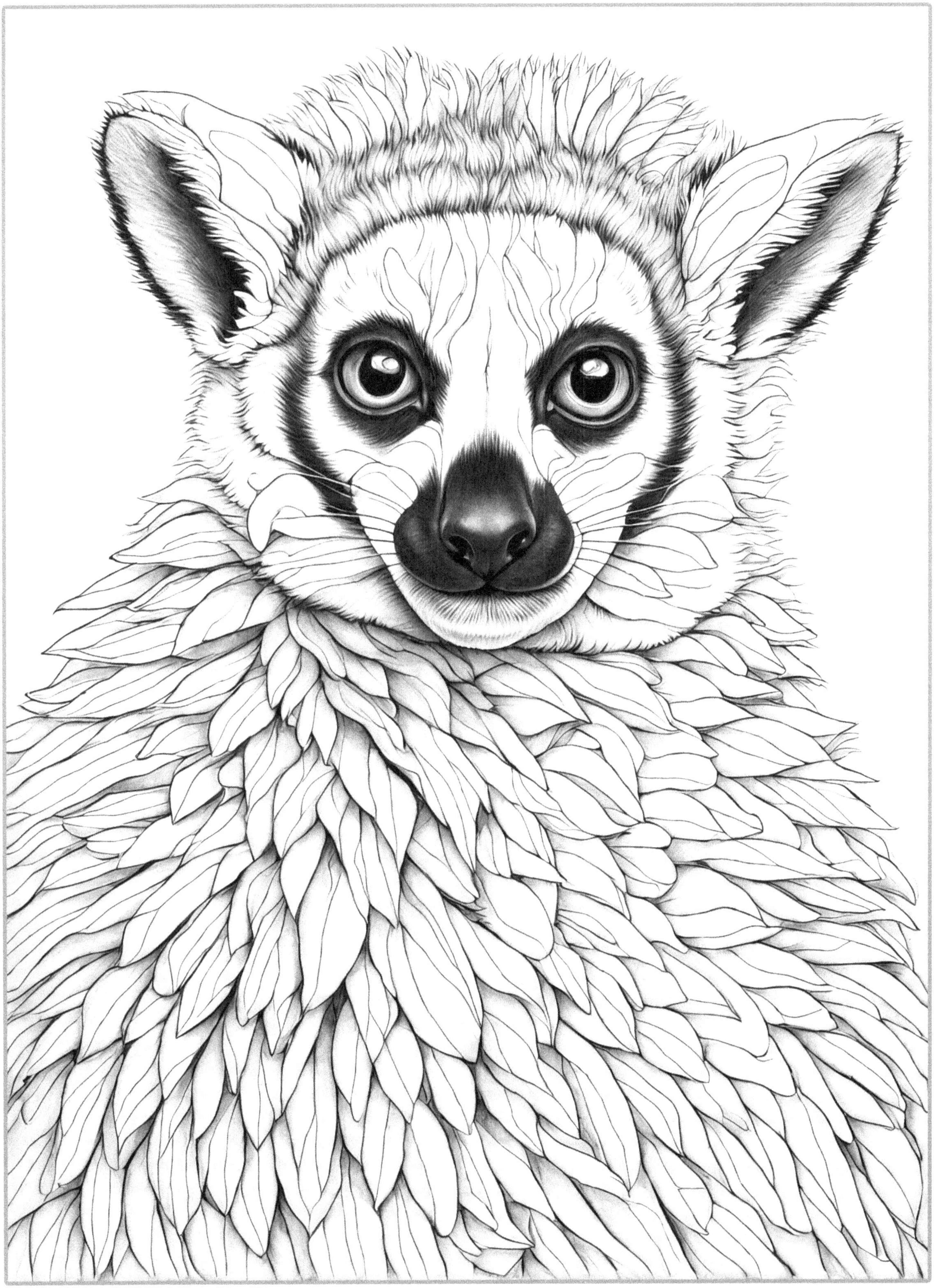

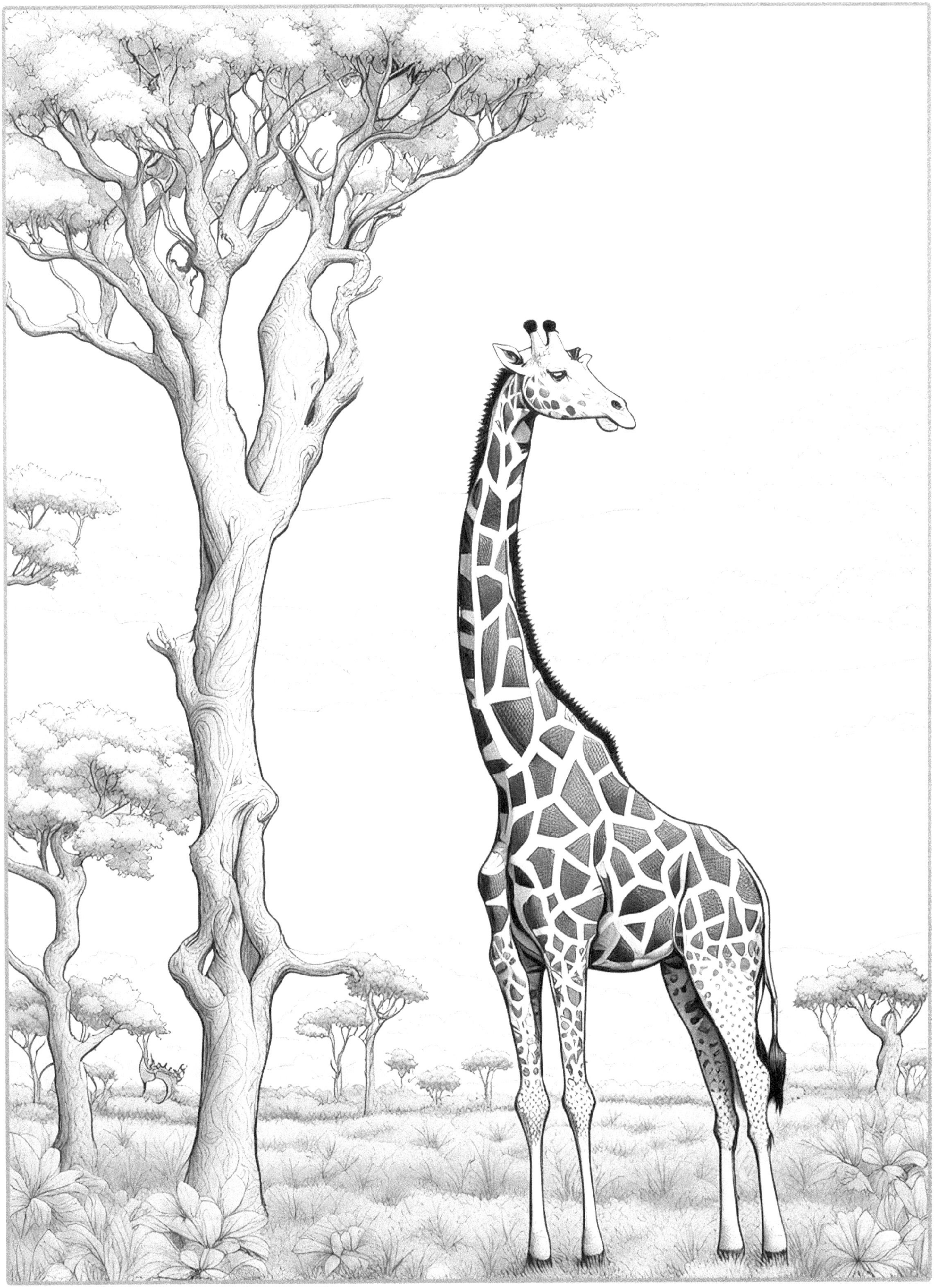

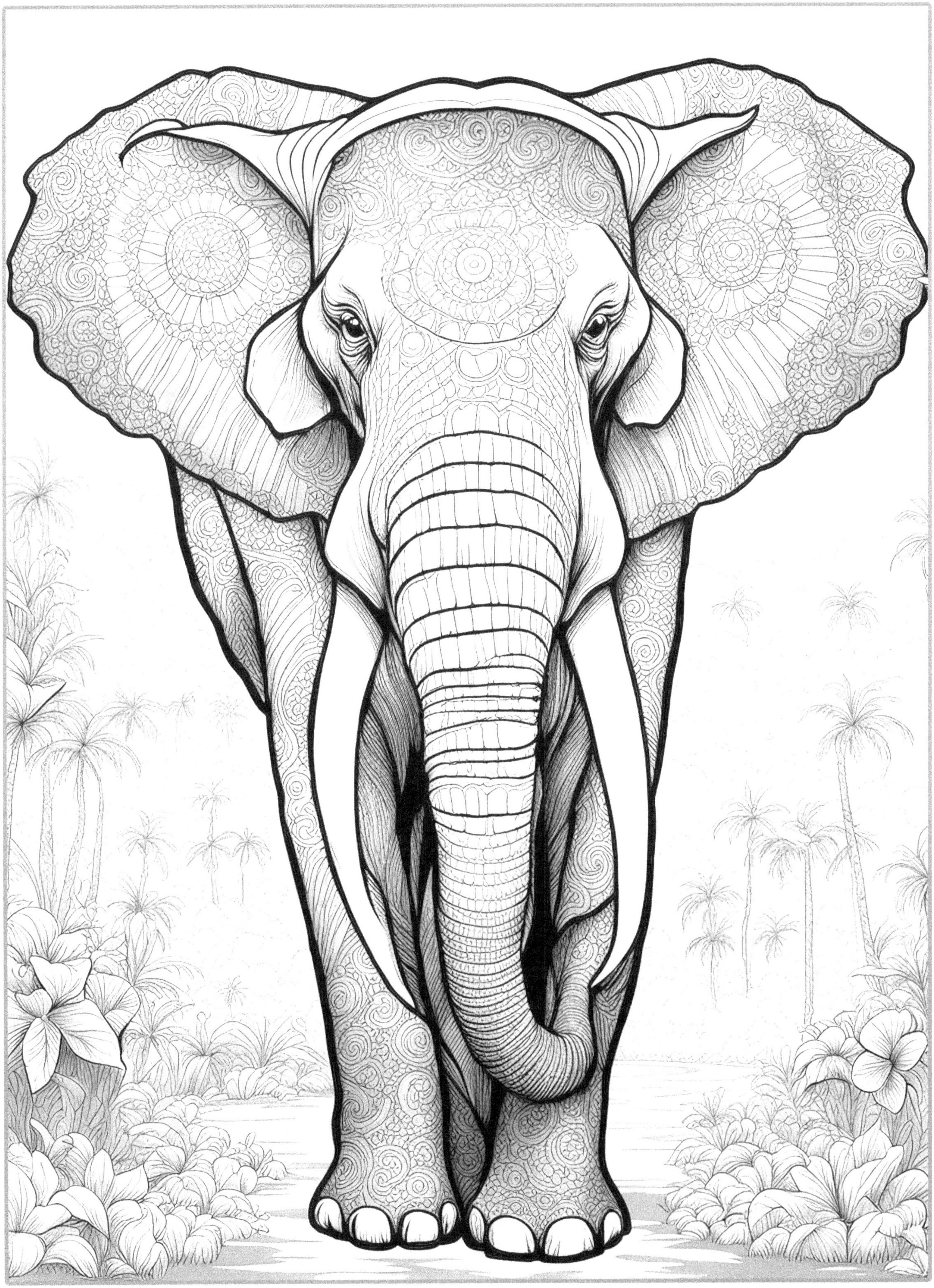

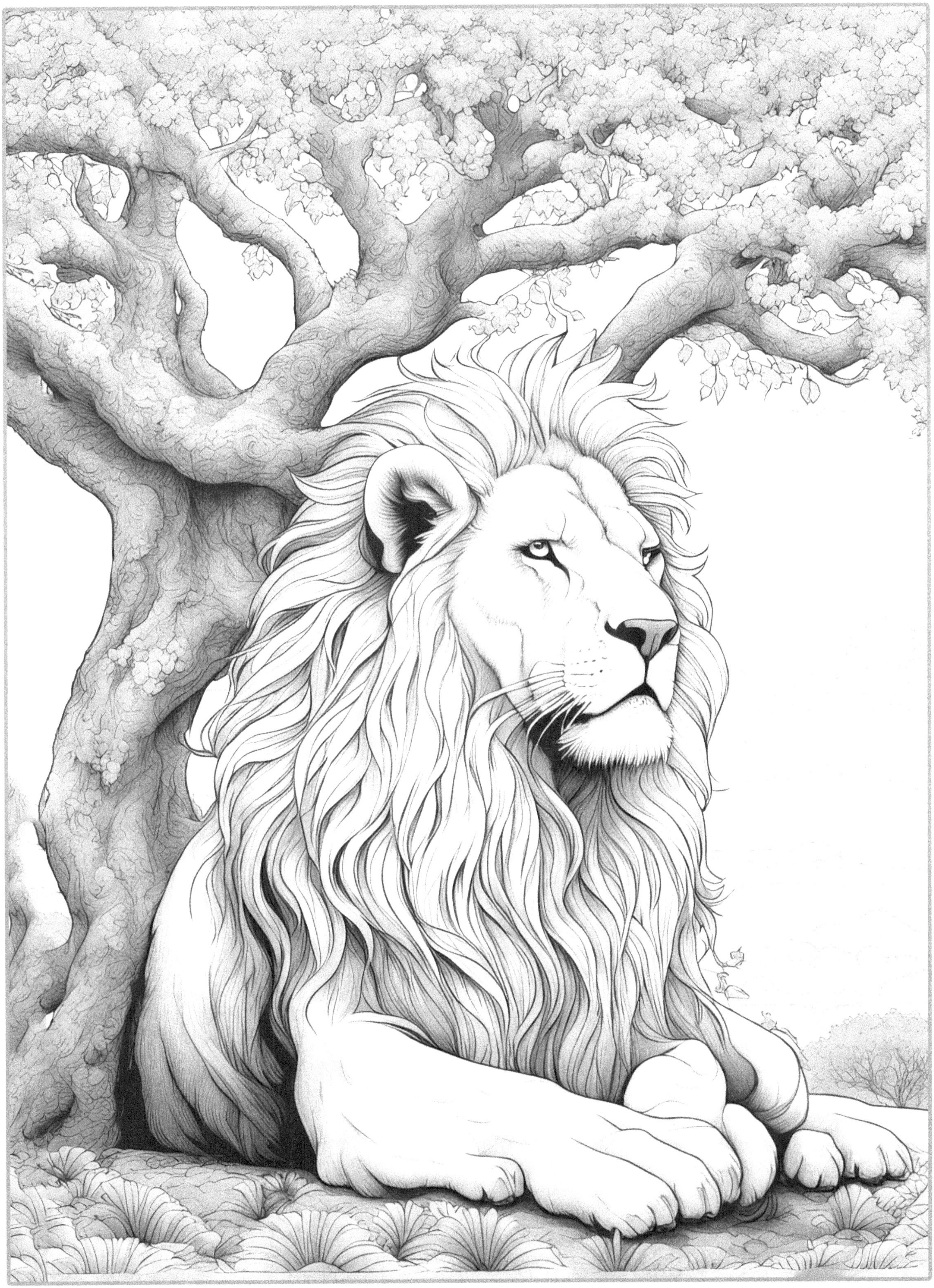

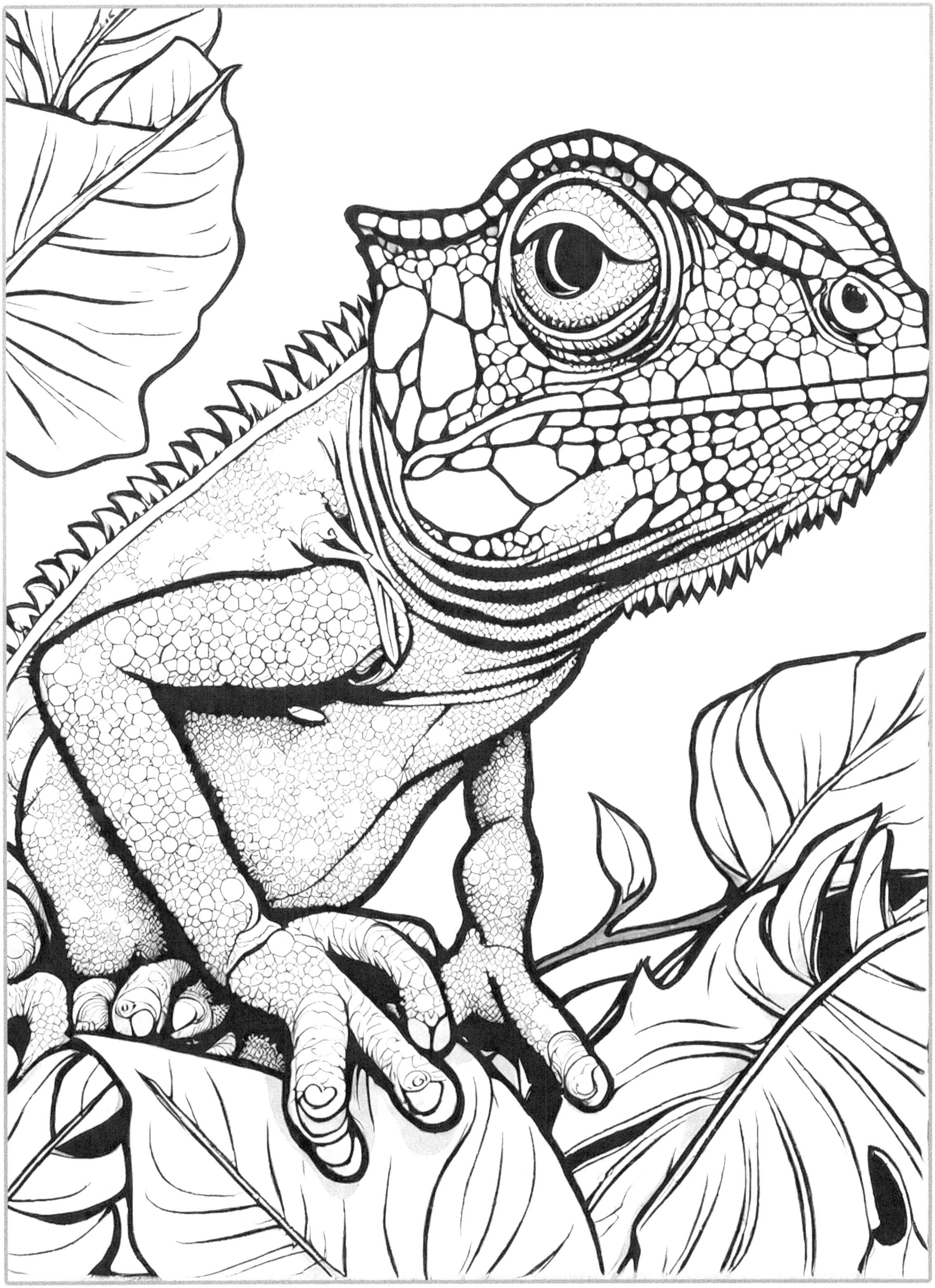

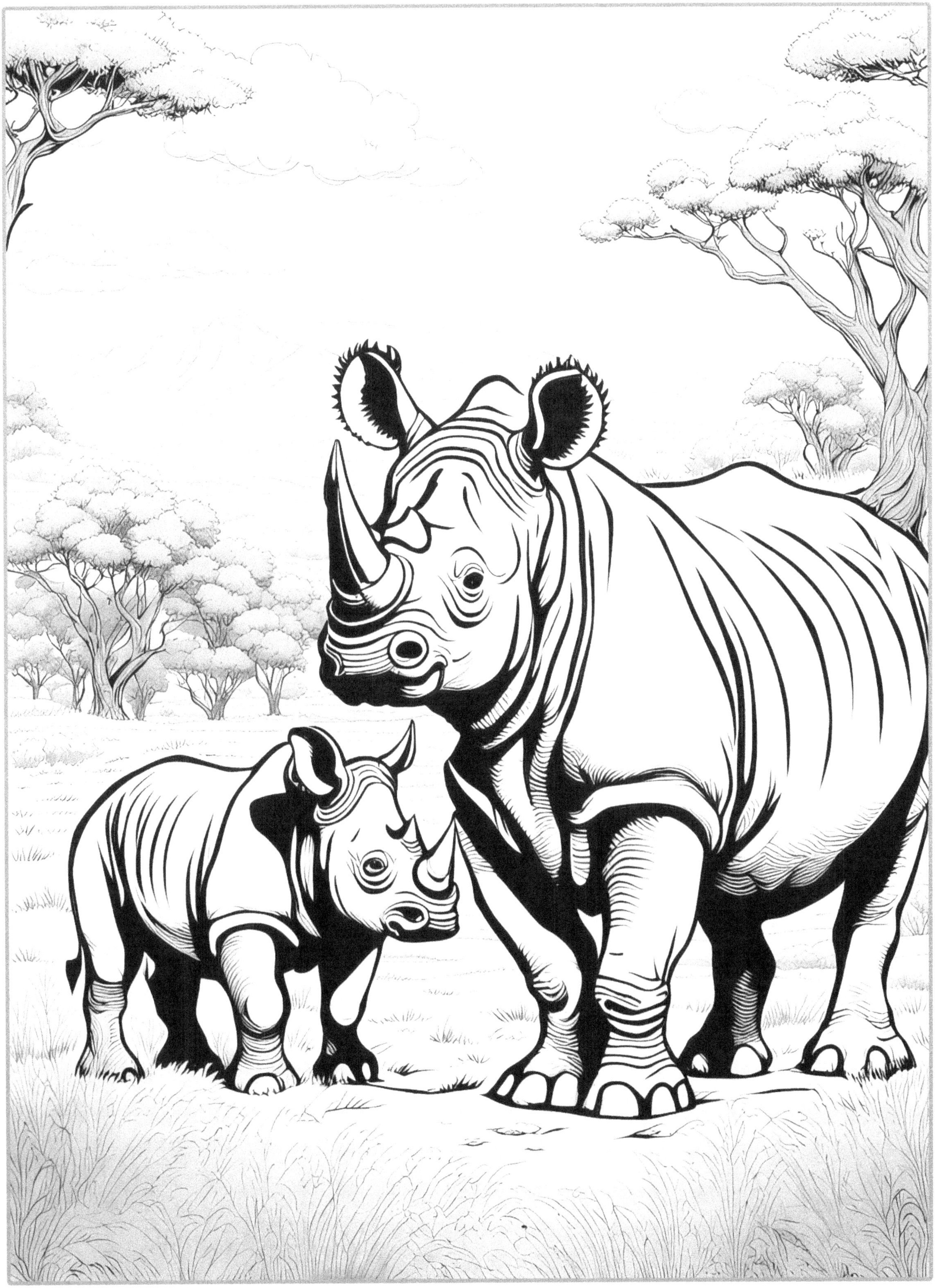

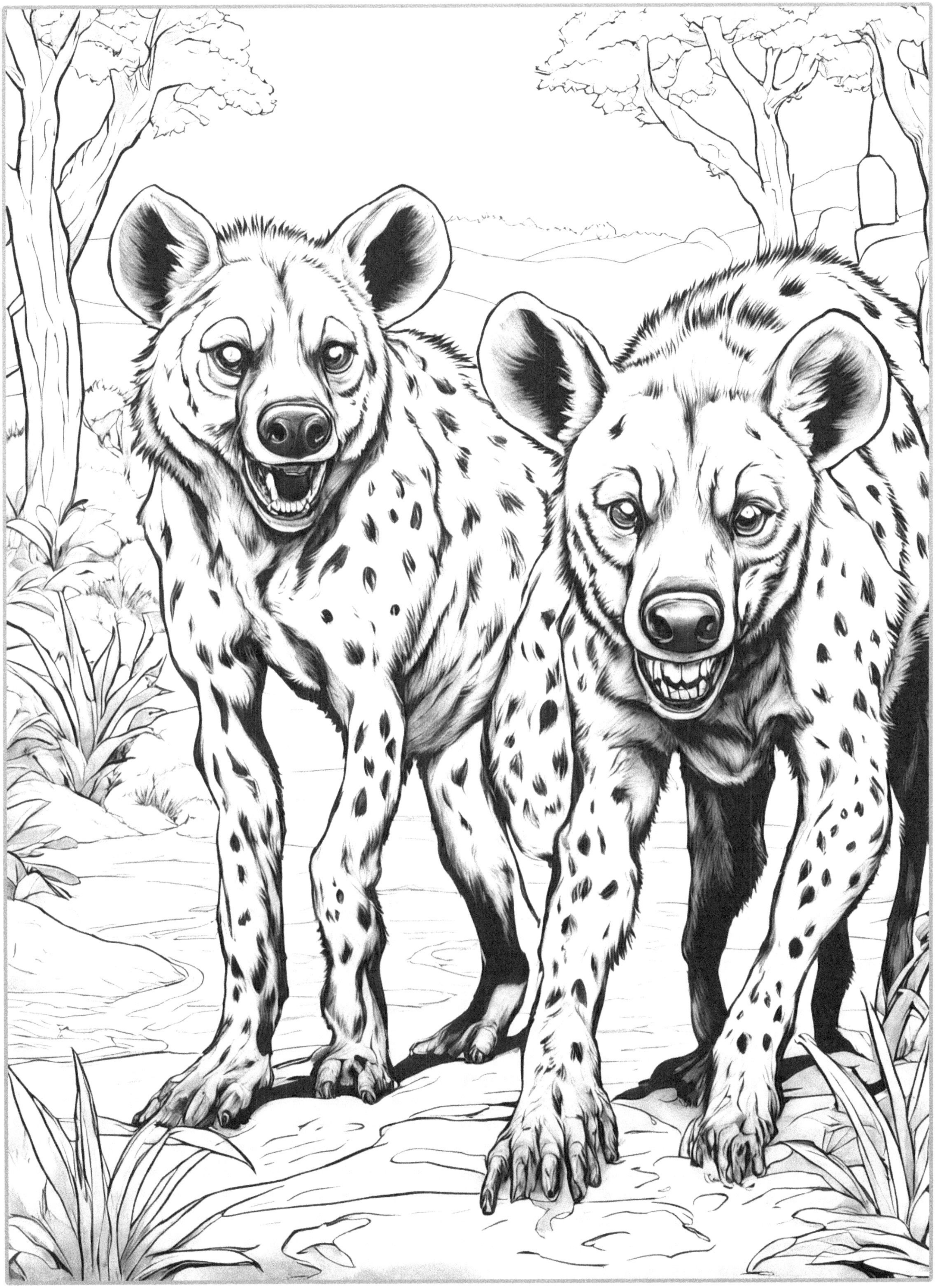

www.ingramcontent.com/pod-product-compliance
Lightning Source LLC
Chambersburg PA
CBHW082217290526
45794CB00009B/3575